G000245703

Simple Cooking at Home

First published in Great Britain in 2016 by

A.R.B Publishing

alan@simplecookingathome.com
www.simplecookingathome.com

Book designer: © 2016 Alan Barnes
Artist and Illustrator: © 2016 Jean Markham
Back cover photography: © 2016 Jon Strange

All rights reserved. No part of this publication
may be reproduced, stored in a retrieval system,
or transmitted in any form or by any means,
electronic, mechanical, photocopying, recording
or otherwise, without prior written permission of the
copyright owner and the above publisher of this book.

A CIP catalogue record for this book is
available from the British Library.

ISBN 978-0-9935314-0-8

Printed and bound in Great Britain by
Orbital Print
Ashford, Kent
TN24 OGA
www.orbitalprint.co.uk

This book is
dedicated to my son
Andrew
with love.

CONTENTS

Acknowledgements

A special thank you to Jean Markham
for all her beautiful illustrations throughout this book.

Also a huge thank you to Ben Cooper
for the layout of the book.

Malcolm Parker
Marnie Summerfield Smith
Rose and John Medlock
for your expertise and encouragement.

Front cover illustrated by Jean Markham
Back cover photography by Jon Strange

Introduction

This is a book compiled from 30 years of cooking over 200 favourite recipes.
I was a great one for collecting recipes, or saving a good menu from a particular hotel or restaurant where I had been currently working.
I always had it in mind to write a cookery book that could be used by everyone, to run with the seasons, using very easy-to-follow recipes.
A week-by-week guide throughout the year giving the most practical advice possible.
To feel as if I were standing beside you in the kitchen, taking you through the recipe.
I have given a three-course menu for each week of the year, with a gentle approach to the preparation, cooking and serving of delicious meals, to give you the enjoyment of preparing a three-course meal, knowing you'll have the confidence to be successful and present good food to your family and friends.
There's a real pleasure and satisfaction in making people happy by cooking them a nice meal.
I hope, by using this book, you will start to create your own menus and enjoy putting ideas together.

The art of good menu writing is:

- To keep it seasonal, with local availability of supplies.

- Avoid repeating the same meat, fish or vegetables in any one menu or repetition of colour.

- Ensure the correct sauces and accompliments are served with the main dishes.

- Write either all in French or English and ensure the spelling is correct

The most important point is to enjoy your cooking and be prepared to make mistakes, we are all still learning. There's not a chef alive that hasn't made a huge mistake, but then went on to perfect that same dish.
A great chef once told me "You're judged on how well you do the simple tasks."

Enjoy simple cooking at home!

ALAN BARNES

Fresh Prawn Cocktail

Heart of a small lettuce.
½ pint peeled cooked prawns.
2 tbsp mayonnaise.
1 tbsp tomato ketchup.
squeeze of lemon juice.
good pinch of salt.
good pinch of cayenne pepper.
lemon wedges.

Wash and dry the lettuce very well, pick out the smaller leaves. Arrange in cocktail glasses and put the prawns on top. Mix the mayonnaise with tomato ketchup, lemon juice and salt. Put over the prawns and garnish with piece of lemon and a dusting of cayenne pepper. **Serve very cold with brown bread and butter.**

Serves 4

Duck Breast with Cherry Sauce

4 Duck Breasts 175-200g each.
drop of vegetable oil.
salt and black pepper.

Heat the oven to 400f 200c gas 6. Sprinkle salt and black pepper on both sides of the duck breasts and score the skin with a sharp knife. In a hot pan suitable for the oven, place the duck skin side down with a drop of oil. When well-browned turn the duck over and put in the oven for 15-18 mins. Remove from the pan and leave to rest in a warm place. **Serve thinly sliced with roast potatoes and carrots.**

Serves 4

Cherry Sauce

1 can of pitted black cherries.
sugar to taste.
2 tbsp redcurrant jelly.
2 tbsp red wine.

Empty the cherries with the juice into a saucepan. Add the sugar, redcurrant jelly and red wine. Heat all the ingredients together and simmer the sauce until the juice is slightly syrupy. Put sauce and cherries around the duck.

Chocolate Cups

300ml double cream.
200g dark chocolate.
20g soft butter.
2 egg yolks.
3 tbsp brandy.

Heat the cream in a small saucepan until nearly boiling. Remove from heat and stir in the broken chocolate pieces and butter until dissolved. Whisk in the egg yolks and brandy until smooth. Pour into espresso cups and chill in the fridge.
Ideal with a biscuit.

Serves 4

Potato and Celeriac Soup

30g butter
1 onion
450g potatoes
1 large celeriac
2 pints vegetable stock
salt and white pepper
1tbsp chopped parsley

Melt the butter in a saucepan. Slice the onion and fry gently in the butter for 5 mins. Peel and slice the potatoes and celeriac, add to the onions and continue to cook gently without colouring. Add the stock, salt and pepper, bring to a boil then simmer for 30 mins. After 30 mins liquidize the soup to a puree, adjust the seasoning and stir in the chopped parsley. **Serve very hot.**

Serves 6

Braised Beefsteak and Onions

700g beefsteak
2 onions
1 carrot
1 turnip
1 leek
2 sticks celery
3 rashers bacon
1 pint brown gravy
salt and pepper
few sprigs of thyme

Peel and dice the onion and all the vegetables. Cut the bacon into strips and make the gravy. Place all the vegetables into a casserole dish, add bacon and thyme. Put the steaks on top and season with salt and pepper. Pour the gravy over to cover the steaks. Cover with a well-fitting lid and cook for 1 ½ hours 350 f 180 c gas 4.
Serve with mashed potato.

Serves 4

Apple Amber

450g cooking apples
1tbsp water
20g butter
50g caster sugar
grated rind and juice of ½ lemon
¼ tsp ground cinnamon
1 tbsp breadcrumbs
2 egg yolks

for the meringue: 2 egg whites, 110g caster sugar

Grease a pint-size pie dish. Peel, core and slice the apples, put them in a saucepan and cook them in the water with butter, sugar, lemon rind and cinnamon. Mash the apples to a pulp, add lemon juice and breadcrumbs. Taste and sweeten if necessary.
When slightly cooled beat in the egg yolks and turn the mixture into the dish.
Bake for 20 mins at 350f 180c gas 4 until just set.
Reduce the oven heat to 275 f 140 c gas 1.
Stiffly whisk the egg whites and fold in 80g of the caster sugar until the meringue is smooth and glossy. Spoon the meringue on top of the apple and smooth it over with a palette knife, sprinkle the remaining sugar over the top of meringue. Bake in a very cool oven until the meringue is golden, about 30 mins. **Serve hot or cold.**

Serves 6.

Chicken Terrine (makes 2 pint loaf tin)

2 Chicken breasts-diced
225g minced pork
275g pork belly fat-minced
175g chicken livers-diced
¾ tsp salt
½ tsp grated nutmeg
1 cloves garlic-chopped
¾ tsp ground black pepper
150 ml dry white wine
1 tbsp brandy
1tsp fresh thyme leaves
175g smoked bacon-chopped

Mix all the ingredients together well. Place inside a greased loaf tin and cover with baking parchment paper, then cover with foil. Place the terrine in a roasting tray and half fill with boiling water and bake in the oven for 2 hours on 300 f 150 c gas 2. Middle shelf. Remove from the oven, allow to cool and leave in the fridge overnight to set.
Serve with hot toast.

Lemon Haddock

700g Fillet of Haddock
1 tbsp olive oil
1 lemon-sliced
juice of 1 lemon
salt and black pepper
2 level tsp cornflour
½ tsp sugar

Cut the lemon into 6 slices. Cut the haddock into four portions for serving and arrange them in a greased dish. Sprinkle with olive oil and a little salt and pepper, add the lemon juice and place the slices of lemon over the top.
Cover with foil and bake in the oven for 15-20 mins on 400 f 200 c gas 6. Strain off the liquid and make up to ¼ pint with water. Blend the cornflour with this, add sugar and bring to the boil, stirring consistantly. Simmer gently for 3 mins. Pour over the fish.

Serves 4

Treacle Tart

First make short crust pastry – see week 3
4 tbsp golden syrup
½ tsp ground ginger
juice of ½ a lemon
6 tbsp fresh brown breadcrumbs

Roll out the pastry on a floured surface to 3 mm thickness and line a greased 9 inch oven plate, trim the edge of any excess pastry. In a saucepan slightly warm the golden syrup, add the ground ginger and lemon juice then stir in the breadcrumbs. Pour the syrup mixture into the pastry case and decorate with thin strips of pastry twisted, to form a criss-cross lattice design. Place the tart on a baking tray in the middle of the oven. Bake for 25-30 mins on 400 f 200 c gas 6 until golden.
Allow to cool. Serve with vanilla ice cream. Serves 6.

Short Crust Pastry

500g plain flour
10g salt
250g butter
1 egg - beaten
75g water

Sieve flour and salt. Rub in the butter until it resembles breadcrumbs. Add the egg and water a little at a time to form a firm dough. Wrap in cling film and rest in the fridge for 30 minutes before using. Use as required. This pastry freezes well.

Sweet Pastry

450g plain flour
220g margarine or butter
100g caster sugar
1 egg – beaten, 55ml milk

Sieve the flour. Rub the margarine or butter into the flour using the finger-tips. Add the sugar and mix in the egg and milk to form a firm dough. Keep dough wrapped in cling film. Rest in the fridge for 30 minutes before using. Use as required.
This pastry freezes well.

Butter-Bean Soup

175g dried butter-beans
2 small onions
2 turnips
2 carrots
2 sticks celery
175g potato
100g butter
2 pints vegetable stock
bunch mixed herbs
pinch salt and pepper

Wash the beans. Soak in boiling water overnight; use this water in the soup. Peel the vegetables and slice them thinly. Melt the butter in a large saucepan and add the sliced vegetables to it, put a lid on and cook gently for 10 mins. Add the stock, beans and herbs. Add salt and pepper and simmer the soup for 1 ½ hours until the vegetables are soft. Liquidize the soup to a puree. **Serve very hot.**

Serves 4.

Meatballs in Tomato Sauce with Spaghetti

125g onion
1 clove garlic
1tbsp oil for frying
450g lean pork mince
100g fresh white breadcrumbs
1 egg- beaten
1 tbsp parsley- chopped
1 tsp salt
½ tsp white pepper

Peel and dice the onion and garlic, gently fry in oil for 5 mins without colouring. Allow to cool.
Mix all the ingredients together in a bowl. With a little flour on your hands, take a small amount and roll it into a ball. Continue rolling until all the mixture has been shaped into meatballs. Put the meatballs onto a baking tray and cook in the oven for 20 mins on 350 f 180 c gas 4.

For the tomato sauce:

1 can chopped tomatoes
1 tbsp tomato puree
¼ pint water
¼ tsp ground ginger
¼ tsp nutmeg
pinch of cayenne pepper
pinch of salt
1 tsp sugar
1 tbsp vinegar

Put all the ingredients in a pan and bring to the boil, simmer for 30 mins. Puree with a hand blender until smooth. Place the cooked meatballs into the tomato sauce and keep warm. Ideal with spaghetti. **Serves 4.**

for the spaghetti:
Allow 75g per person. Add the pasta to a large pan of slightly salted boiling water, stir and return to the boil. Cook for 10 mins, drain well.

Meringue Coconut Shells

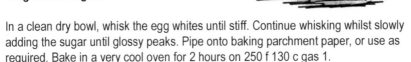

Plain meringue:
2 egg whites.
110g caster sugar.

In a clean dry bowl, whisk the egg whites until stiff. Continue whisking whilst slowly adding the sugar until glossy peaks. Pipe onto baking parchment paper, or use as required. Bake in a very cool oven for 2 hours on 250 f 130 c gas 1.

Coconut meringues:
2 egg whites
150g caster sugar
100g desiccated coconut

Whisk the egg whites and sugar as for plain meringue, then fold in the coconut with a spatula. Put the mixture into a piping bag with a star nozzle. Pipe small rosettes onto baking parchment paper, dredge them at once with sugar and put them in the oven to bake without browning for 1 hour on 250 f 130 c gas 1. When dry and cool, sandwich 2 shells together with whipped cream or ice cream. Shells can be half dipped in melted chocolate, allowed to set then sandwiched together with cream.

Sea-food Chowder

1 smoked haddock about 500g
1 onion-sliced
1 potato-diced
2 tomatoes
30g butter
1 tbsp plain flour
4 tbsp double cream
pinch salt and pepper
½ pint cooked and peeled prawns
50g peas
1 tbsp chopped parsley

Put the haddock in a pan and cover with water. Bring slowly to the boil and simmer for 5 mins. Remove from heat and skim off scum from stock. Set the haddock to one side and cook the onions in the stock until soft. Add the potato and cook until soft. Skin the tomatoes and cut in quarters and remove the seeds, then dice the tomato. Put the tomato into the stock with the onion and potato. Skin and bone the haddock. Melt the butter in another pan and add the flour, stir together and cook for 2mins without browning. Slowly stir in the liquid from the vegetables and add the cream. Add salt and pepper, vegetables, flakes of haddock and prawns. Add the peas and parsley, **serve hot. Serves 4.**

Shepherd's Pie

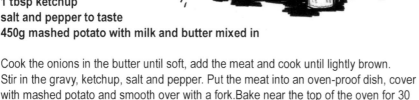

2 onions-diced
75g butter
350g cooked lamb-minced
¼ pint gravy
1 tbsp ketchup
salt and pepper to taste
450g mashed potato with milk and butter mixed in

Cook the onions in the butter until soft, add the meat and cook until lightly brown. Stir in the gravy, ketchup, salt and pepper. Put the meat into an oven-proof dish, cover with mashed potato and smooth over with a fork.Bake near the top of the oven for 30 mins on 425 f 210 c gas 7 until golden brown
Serves 4.

Bread and Butter Pudding

8-10 thin slices of bread and butter
125g sultanas
4 eggs
75g caster sugar
1½ pints milk
1 tsp mixed spice
brown sugar sprinkled on top

Grease a 2 pint pie-dish. Cut the bread into squares and place them neatly in the dish. Sprinkle the first layer with half of the sultanas and a little sugar. Place a second layer of bread on top with the remaining sultanas and a little more sugar. Finish with a top layer, only sprinkle brown sugar on top.
Beat the eggs, milk and mixed spice together, pour over the bread.
Leave to soak for 30 mins. Bake in the oven for 1 hour on 350 f 180 c gas 4 until the custard is set.

Serves 6.

Mussels in White Wine

4 pints of Mussels
1 shallot-finely chopped
¼ pint white wine
30g butter
1tsp chopped parsley

Wash the mussels in cold water, pull away the beards. Discard any broken or open mussels.

In a large saucepan, put the chopped shallot, white wine and mussels and cover with a lid. Place over high heat and cook for 5 mins, shaking the pan now and again, until all the mussels have opened.

Remove the pan from the heat and take out the mussels, discarding any that have not opened. Return the pan to the heat, add the butter and boil for a further 5 mins, add the chopped parsley and a pinch of salt and pepper.

Remove the half of the shell with the mussel still inside and arrange in bowls. Pour the hot liquid over the mussels in the bowls. **Serve at once.**
Serves 4.

Pork, roast

Weigh the joint and calculate the cooking time, 30-35 mins per lb and 30 mins over.
For small joints 360f 180c gas4.
Joints over 5 lb, 380f 190c gas5.
Rub salt all over the skin for really good cracking. Baste during cooking with hot fat.
Suitable joints for roasting – loin, leg, hand and spring, blade, spare rib.
Serves 4.

Apple Sauce

900g cooking apples
60g butter
sugar to taste

Peel, core and quarter apples. Cook in a little water for 10 mins until soft, mash to a pulp. Add butter and sugar to taste. **Serve hot or cold.**

Apricot and Nut Stuffing

120g dried apricots
2 onions-sliced
50g butter
90g sultanas
60g chopped nuts
100g breadcrumbs
grated rind and juice of 1 lemon
salt and pepper

Soak apricots for 1 hour in hot water, drain and finely chop. Fry the onions in the butter until golden brown, add sultanas and nuts. Cook for a further few minutes, then turn into a bowl.
Add all the other ingredients, mix with a fork. Put in an oven-proof dish.
Bake for 20 mins on 350f 180c gas 4. Use as required.

Thickened Gravy

After joint has been removed, strain off all but one tablespoon of fat, leaving juices and sediment behind. Add 1 tbsp of flour, mix in well and stir over a gentle heat until brown. Add 1 pint stock and boil for 5 mins, season to taste. Strain. Pour into a gravy boat and serve hot.

Strawberry Jam Sponge

3 tbsp of strawberry jam
125g butter
125g caster sugar
2 eggs
125g plain flour
5g baking powder
desiccated coconut to decorate

Grease and flour a small loaf tin. Preheat the oven to 350f 180c gas4.
Spoon the strawberry jam into the bottom of the tin. Beat the butter and sugar together until creamy. Mix in the eggs, followed by the flour and baking powder. Mix well, fill the tin with the cake mixture and bake for 35-40 mins. Turn out the sponge onto a serving dish, so the jam is on the top, sprinkle coconut over the jam. **Serve hot with custard. Serves 4.**

Onion Soup with Crunchy Croutons

3 large spanish onions
30g butter
30g flour
1 pint of stock-warm
½ pint of milk
1 clove
1 bayleaf
salt and pepper

Peel and thinly slice the onions. Melt the butter in a large saucepan and lightly fry the onions for 10 mins without colouring. Stir in the flour, mix in the warm stock. Add the clove, bayleaf and simmer for 30 mins until the onions are tender. Add the milk and cook until the soup thickens. Salt and pepper to taste. **Serve with crunchy croutons.**
Serves 4.

Crunchy Croutons

1 ciabatta roll, olive oil, salt.
Cut the bread into small squares (approx 1 cm) including the crusts.
Lay them out on a baking tray and drizzle with olive oil and sprinkle with salt. Bake in the oven on 400f 200c gas 6 turning often for 15 mins. Drain on to absorbent paper.
Will keep fresh for 3 days in an air-tight container. **Serve with soups and salads.**

Chicken in Red Wine Sauce

1 whole chicken 1.6-2kg
30g flour - seasoned
30g butter   1tbsp oil
2 cloves garlic - crushed
3 sprigs thyme
1 onion - sliced
100g button mushrooms
2 rashers of bacon
1 pint red wine.   ½ pint brown gravy
salt and pepper (continued on next page)

Chicken in Red Wine Sauce (continued)

Method: Chicken in Red Wine Sauce.
Ask the butcher to cut the chicken into eight pieces, so you will have two breasts each cut in half, two thighs and two drumsticks. Lightly flour and season each piece of chicken. Melt the butter and a little oil together in a frying pan, seal and colour the chicken on both sides quickly. Remove the chicken and place them into a casserole dish with the crushed garlic and thyme. Put the frying pan back on the heat and fry the sliced onion, mushrooms and strips of bacon in the chicken fat until lightly browned.
Put this over the chicken in the casserole. Pour the red wine over the chicken together with the gravy, salt and pepper. Cover with a tight-fitting lid and cook in the oven for 1 hour on 300f 150c gas 3, until the chicken is tender. Middle shelf. **Serves 4.**

Valentine's Chocolate Cake

125g butter
2 eggs
1 tsp baking powder
25g cocoa powder.
1tsp instant coffee.

125g caster sugar
100g plain flour

pinch of salt
1tbsp milk

Beat the butter and sugar together until creamy. Scrap down the bowl, mix in the eggs, flour, baking powder, cocoa powder and salt. Dissolve the coffee in a little tepid milk and stir in to bind. Line a 7in cake tin with baking parchment paper and pour in the mixture. Bake for 40 mins on 375f 190c gas 5. Middle shelf. To test, insert a wooden skewer into the centre of the cake, if it comes out clean its cooked properly. If not, return the cake to the oven for a further 5 mins. When cooked, remove from the tin and allow to cool on a wire rack. When the cake is cold, cut through the middle to make two halves, spread whipped cream and jam on both sides and sandwich back together. Place back on the wire rack over a tray, pour the chocolate glaze over the cake, top and sides. Smooth out with a palette knife, allow to set in the fridge. When the glaze is completely set transfer the cake to a nice serving plate. Write Happy Valentine's Day on the top in melted white chocolate or decorate as you wish. **Serves 6.**

Chocolate Glaze

125 ml milk, 50 ml double cream, 250g dark chocolate, 65g soft butter
Break up the chocolate into a metal bowl. In a small saucepan boil the milk and cream together, pour it over the chocolate stirring until dissolved. Whisk in the soft butter until smooth and shiny. Use to cover cakes and desserts.

Chicken and Leek Soup

2 chicken breasts 2 chicken thighs, both on the bone
1 large potato
500g leeks
3 sprigs of thyme
salt and pepper
1 tbsp of chopped parsley
dash of cream

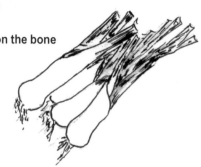

Wash the chicken pieces in cold water. Put the chicken in a saucepan and cover with cold water.
Bring slowly to simmering point, add 2 tsp of salt and simmer for 45 mins. Meanwhile, peel and dice the potato, wash and trim the leeks, cutting them into thin rings. Add the potato, leeks and thyme after it has been simmering for 45 mins, continue cooking for a further 45 mins.
After 1 ½ hours lift out the chicken pieces. Cut the meat away from the bone and cut into small cubes, return these to the soup. Add salt and pepper if needed, before serving stir in the chopped parsley and a dash of cream in each bowl.

Serves 4.

Pancake Recipes

Savoury Pancakes:

120g wholemeal flour
½ tsp salt
2 eggs
½ pint water

Sieve the flour and salt into a bowl, whisk in the eggs and water to form a smooth batter. Leave to stand for 30 mins before using.

Filling suggestions:
Ham, cheese and tomato. Mushrooms in white sauce.
Prawns and haddock in cheese sauce.

Sweet Pancakes:

120 plain flour
pinch of salt
1 egg
½ pint milk

Sieve the flour and salt into a bowl, whisk in the egg and milk to form a smooth batter. Leave to stand for 30 mins before using.

Filling suggestions:
Lemon and sugar. Chocolate fudge or toffee sauce.
Spiced apples with whisky cream.

Carrot and Celeriac Salad

2 large carrots
1 celeriac
1 apple
2 tbsp of sour cream
salt and pepper
crisp lettuce hearts
8 slices of parma ham
mustard and cress for decoration

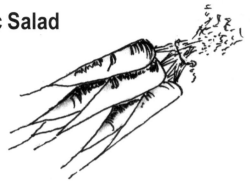

Peel the carrots, celeriac and apple, finely shred into thin strips. Mix them together in a bowl with enough sour cream to bind, add salt and pepper to taste.
Wash, drain and dry the lettuce leaves, arrange neatly on plates.
Spoon the mixture onto the leaves and place the parma ham on the sides, allowing two slices per person.
Finish with mustard and cress.

Serves 4.

Chicken Casserole

500g chicken – diced
2 tbsp flour
1 onion
1 carrot
1parsnip
1 pint of stock
3 sprigs of thyme
salt and pepper
1 tbsp chopped parsley

Coat the chicken pieces in flour and place them into a casserole dish. Peel and slice the onion, carrot and parsnip, add them to the casserole dish. Pour over the stock, add the thyme and season with salt and pepper. Cook in the oven for 1 hour on 350f 180c gas 4 with a tight-fitting lid, stirring halfway. Middle shelf. Sprinkle with chopped parsley and **serve hot.**

Serves 4.

Rhubarb Crumble

500g prepared rhubarb
1 tbsp water
120g brown sugar
grated rind and juice of 1 orange

To prepare the rhubarb, cut off the leaves and thick ends of the sticks. Wipe the sticks with a damp cloth, cut into 2 inch lengths. Put the rhubarb, water and sugar into an oven-proof dish, grate the orange rind over the fruit and cover with foil.
Bake in the oven for 20 mins on 325f 160c gas 3 until the fruit is just soft.
Add the orange juice once the rhubarb is cooked. Set aside.

For the crumble :

150g self-raising flour
75g butter
60g caster sugar
½ tsp mixed spice
brown sugar to sprinkle on top

Sieve the flour into a bowl. Rub in the butter until it resembles breadcrumbs, blend in the caster sugar and mixed spice. Cover the rhubarb with the crumble and sprinkle a little brown sugar on top.
Bake for 30-40 mins on 350f 180c gas 4 until golden.

Serves 4.

Leek and Potato Soup

500g leeks
500g potatoes
30g butter
1 pint stock
½ pint milk
salt and pepper
dash of cream
1 tbsp chopped parsley

Clean the leeks thoroughly, trim and slice them. Peel and dice the potatoes. In a large saucepan melt the butter and fry the leeks for 10 mins. Add the potatoes and stock, bring to the boil and simmer for 30 mins until the potatoes are soft. Liquidize the soup until smooth puree, return to the pan, add the milk, salt and pepper to taste, reheat. Add the cream, chopped parsley and **serve into bowls.**

Serves 6.

Leg of Lamb, roast

Allow 20 mins per lb and 20 mins extra for roasting
1 leg of lamb-boned and rolled
1 onion
1 carrot
2 cloves garlic
salt and pepper
a little oil
sprig of fresh rosemary

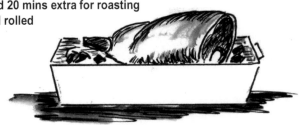

Ask the butcher for a leg of lamb-boned and rolled, size depending on how many people you are serving. Peel and slice the onion and carrot, crush the garlic. Put them into a roasting tin and sit the lamb on top, so the joint is resting on the vegetables and not touching the tin. Season the meat with salt and pepper, drizzle a little oil over the top and sprigs of rosemary. Bake at 400f 200c gas 6.
(Thickened gravy – see week 6)

Egg Custard Tart
(Make sweet pastry dough – see week 3)

For the custard filling:
9 egg yolks
90g caster sugar
500ml whipping cream
freshly grated nutmeg

Roll out the pastry on a floured surface to 3mm thickness. Line a greased 8in flan case with the pastry and trim the edges, place on a baking tray and put a circle of baking parchment paper inside the pastry case, slightly over-lapping. Fill it with baking beans or uncooked rice {this is called "baking blind"}. Bake for 20 mins on 375f 190c gas 5, second shelf from top, until the pastry starts to turn golden. Remove the paper and beans, brush a little egg yolk inside the pastry case to completely coat it, return to the oven for 3 mins. This will create a seal to prevent the tart from leaking. Set aside.
Turn the oven down to 330f 160c gas 3. Whisk together the egg yolks and sugar, add the cream and mix well. Fill the pastry case with the custard until 5 mm from the top. Carefully place on the middle shelf of the oven and bake for 20-30 mins, until the custard is set. Remove from the oven and lightly cover the surface with grated nutmeg. Allow to cool to room temperature. **Serves 6.**

Garlic Mushrooms on Toast

First make the garlic butter – see week 11
225g button mushrooms
120g garlic butter
150ml double cream
salt and pepper
4 thick slices of bread

Brush the mushrooms clean to remove any dirt. Melt the garlic butter in a pan, fry the mushrooms for 10 mins until brown. Pour in the cream and cook for a further 5 mins until the cream starts to thicken and coats the mushrooms in sauce. Add salt and pepper to taste. Meanwhile toast the bread and remove the crusts. Spoon the mushrooms and sauce over the toast, **serve at once.**

Serves 6.

Garlic Butter

120g butter- soft
4 cloves garlic
1tsp lemon juice
1tbsp olive oil
1tbsp chopped parsley

Peel and finely chop the garlic, blend into the butter. Add the lemon juice, olive oil and parsley. Mix in thoroughly and use as required.

Baked Potatoes

Choose four evenly sized potatoes.
Wash, dry and lightly rub a little oil over the skins, sprinkle with salt.
Place onto a baking tray and cook for 1½ hours on 375f 190c gas 5. Middle shelf.

Chicken Breasts, fried

4 chicken breasts- 175-200g each
2tbsp flour
salt and pepper
pinch of paprika
2 eggs-beaten
white breadcrumbs
oil for frying

Coat the chicken in flour which has been sieved with salt, pepper and paprika. Then dip into the beaten egg, then into the breadcrumbs. Heat the oil in a shallow pan, gently fry the chicken for about 10 mins on both sides, until cooked through. Drain onto absorbent paper, **serve with baked potatoes.**

Serves 4.

Fresh Fruit Salad

Make a stock syrup with 225g caster sugar and ½ pint of water.
Put the sugar and water into a small saucepan, bring to the boil stirring to ensure all the sugar has dissolved. Continue to boil for 1 minute, remove from the heat and allow to completely cool.
Choose a ripe melon, pineapple, grapes, apples and oranges. Skin and cut the melon and pineapple into cubes. Cut the grapes in half lengthways, slice the apples and oranges removing any pips.
Mix the fruit together in a serving bowl and pour over the cold syrup.
Refrigerate until ready to serve.

Serves 6.

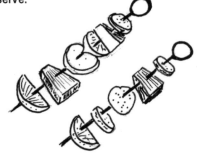

King Prawns in Garlic Butter

First make the garlic butter - see week 11
12 king prawns
squeeze of lemon juice
lemon wedges

Allow 6 king prawns per person. Melt the garlic butter in a large frying pan, gently fry all the prawns for 4 mins on both sides until they turn pink. Just before serving squeeze the lemon juice over the prawns. Serve at once with a little of the hot butter and a lemon wedge on the side.

Serves 2.

Irish Stew

900g lamb - best end of neck
900g potatoes
6 onions
1 pint of stock
salt and pepper
1 tbsp chopped parsley

Divide the meat into cutlets or pieces.
Arrange in a saucepan in layers, with the thickly-sliced onions, salt, pepper and half the potatoes sliced.
Add the stock and simmer with a tight-fitting lid on the hob for 1 hour. Cover the meat in the remainder of the potatoes, which have been cut into large dice. Simmer for 45 mins until potatoes on top are tender but unbroken.
Serve with the potatoes around the meat, sprinkle with chopped parsley.

Serves 4.

Potato Scones

250g potatoes
¼ tsp of salt
15g butter
60g self-raising flour

Cook the potatoes in salted water until soft, drain and mash well. Add salt and butter. Work in the flour with a wooden spoon to form a pliable paste which can be rolled out, without sticking. Roll out very thinly on a floured surface. Cut into rounds with a 6cm pastry cutter and cook on a gridle or a dry non-stick frying pan, for 3 mins on each side until golden. **Serve hot with butter.**

Serves 4.

Chocolate Brownie

275g dark chocolate 70%
225g butter
400g caster sugar
1tsp vanilla essence
pinch of salt
5eggs
200g plain flour
100g walnut pieces (optional)

Heat the oven to 300f 150c gas 2. Break the chocolate into small pieces together with the diced butter into a metal bowl. Place the bowl over a saucepan of simmering water on the hob. When the chocolate and butter are melted, whisk in the sugar, vanilla essence and salt. Remove from the heat and add the eggs one at a time, mixing in each one before adding the next. Stir in the sieved flour with a large metal spoon, until all the flour has been mixed in properly. Finally stir in the walnuts. Line a 10in x 12in baking tray, with baking parchment paper and pour the mixture into the tray. Bake for 30-35 mins until the outside is set but soft in the middle. Second shelf from top. Allow to cool, cut into squares.

Serves 12.

Poached Eggs on Spinach

400g spinach leaves
30g butter
freshly grated nutmeg
pinch salt and pepper
4 eggs
½ pint of cheese sauce

Prepare and cook the spinach:
Remove and discard the stalks from the spinach leaves, wash and dry the leaves well, cut into strips. In a small saucepan, melt the butter and quickly cook the spinach leaves for 3-4 mins, add grated nutmeg, salt and pepper. Drain any excess water from the spinach, keep warm.

For the cheese sauce:

½ pint of warm milk
30g butter,
30g flour
pinch of salt and white pepper
60g grated cheddar cheese

In a saucepan, melt the butter. Stir in the flour with a wooden spoon, gradually add the warm milk stirring until it has all been mixed in. Add salt and pepper and simmer gently for 20 mins, then stir in the cheese, keep warm. **Serves 4.**

To poach the egg:

Put a shallow pan on the hob, half filled with water, a dash of vinegar and a pinch of salt, bring to the boil. When the water and vinegar have come to the boil, turn down to low and crack an egg into the simmering water and poach the egg for 3 mins, lift out and drain.
To serve: Place a spoonful of spinach in the centre of a warm plate, sit the poached egg on top of the spinach and pour some cheese sauce over the egg, just enough to cover. **Serve at once.**
Serves 4.

Chicken and Leek pie

Make short crust pasrty-see week 3
600g cooked chicken-diced
60g butter
120g leeks-sliced
1 onion- diced
60g flour
1 pint of stock
100ml double cream
salt and pepper

In a saucepan melt the butter, gently cook the leeks and onion for 10 mins. Stir in the flour and mix in well. Gradually add the stock until it forms a smooth sauce, simmer for 20 mins. Add cream, salt and pepper. Mix in the chicken, allow to cool.
Roll out the pastry on a floured surface to 3mm thickness and line a greased oven-proof plate with the pastry and trim the edges. Roll out a second piece slightly larger than the plate. Spoon the chicken onto the pastry lined plate; moisten the edge with a little beaten egg. Place the second piece of pastry over the chicken and crimp down by pinching the edges to seal. Trim around the edges and make a hole in the centre of the lid for the steam to escape.Decorate with leaves cut from the trimmings. Brush beaten egg over the pie and bake for 30-40 mins on 400f 200c gas 6 until golden.
Serves 4.

Vanilla Cheesecake-baked

600g soft cream cheese
45g caster sugar
15g cornflour
2 eggs
3 egg yolks
100ml cream
vanilla seeds from 1 pod

Line the bottom of a 7in cake tin with a thin layer of cooked sponge, (see swiss roll recipe – week 22). Whisk all the ingredients together in a bowl. Pour the mixture onto the sponge base and bake for 30-40 mins on 300f 150c gas 2 until set. Allow to cool slightly, remove from cake tin, **serve warm.**
Serves 4-5.

Pea and Ham Soup

90g dried yellow split peas
1 onion
1 carrot
1 potato
60g butter
1 pint stock
3 rashers of bacon
fresh herbs
pinch of pepper
120g cooked chopped ham

Wash the split peas and soak them in ½ pint of cold water overnight, use this water in the soup. Peel and slice the vegetables. In a large saucepan, melt the butter and cook all the sliced vegetables for 10 mins. Add the stock, split peas, sliced bacon, herbs and pepper. Simmer for 1 ½ hours stirring occasionally, until the vegetables are soft. Liquidize the soup to a smooth puree. **Serve with a little chopped ham on top.**
Serves 4

Salmon in Puff Pastry

4 salmon steaks-175g each
salt and black pepper
500g puff pastry-frozen
1 beaten egg
lemon juice and slices

Ask the fishmonger to skin and cut the salmon into steaks, season each one with salt, pepper and lemon juice. Cut the puff pastry into four equal pieces, roll out each piece on a floured surface to a rectangle-12cm x 15cm. Take the first piece of pastry and place the salmon in the centre, brush a little egg around the edges and fold the pastry over the fish, tuck in the short ends neatly and seal with more egg. Put the salmon on a baking tray, with the seam underneath. Repeat until all salmon is wrapped, decorate with fish cut from the trimmings. Brush with remaining egg. Bake for 35-40 mins on 400f 200c gas 6 until pastry is golden. **Serve hot or cold with lemon slices.**

Serves 4

Golden Syrup Sponge

175g plain flour
175g white breadcrumbs
120g vegetable suet
60g sugar
1tsp ground ginger
1tsp bicarbonate soda
pinch of salt
1 egg
3 tbsp golden syrup
milk to bind

Butter a basin and put 1tbsp of golden syrup in the bottom. Mix together the flour, breadcrumbs, suet, sugar, ginger, bicarbonate soda and salt. Beat the egg with 2 tbsp golden syrup and a little milk.
Stir this into the other ingredients, mix to a dropping consistency, add more milk if required. Put the mixture into the basin; cover with greased paper. Steam for 1 ½ – 2 hours. **Serve with custard.**

Serves 6

Happy Easter!

Welsh Rarebit

175g grated cheddar cheese
3 egg yolks
salt and pepper
2tbsp milk
6 slices of bread

Mix together the cheese, egg yolks, salt, pepper and milk. Toast the slices of bread on one side, on the other side lightly spread the cheese mixture. Place them on a baking tray and put under a medium grill until golden brown. **Serve at once.**
Serves 3-4

Kebabs with Rice

450g Basmati rice
½ tsp salt
450g leg of lamb- cut into 1in cubes
16 cherry tomatoes
8 rashers streaky bacon
175g button mushrooms
16 cocktail sausages
1 tin pineapple chunks
vegetable oil
8 wooden skewers

Ask the butcher for leg of lamb-diced. Wash the rice twice in cold water. Cook the rice in 900ml of boiling, salted water for 12-14 mins, turn off and leave to stand with a lid on. Wash tomatoes and mushrooms, remove rind from bacon, cut each rasher in half and roll up. Drain pineapple. Arrange all ingredients on skewers, brush each kebab with a little vegetable oil and season with salt and pepper. Place the kebabs on a baking tray and place under a hot grill for 10 mins, turning halfway. Spread the rice out on a large serving dish, place kebabs on the bed of rice. 2 kebabs per person.

Serves 4

Carrot Cake

200ml sunflower oil
240g caster sugar
3 eggs
160g plain flour-sifted
1½ tsp baking powder
½ tsp cinnamon
½ tsp ground cloves
¼ tsp salt
200g grated carrot
90g walnut pieces

Mix together the oil and sugar. Whisk in the eggs, add the flour, baking powder, cinnamon, cloves and salt. Stir in the grated carrot and walnuts. Pour into a greased 8in cake tin and bake for 1 hour on 330f 170c gas 3. Middle shelf.
Allow to cool on a wire rack. When cold, spread cinnamon frost over the top.

For the Cinnamon Frost

125g soft butter
250g icing sugar
125g soft cream cheese
4g cinnamon

Cream together the butter and sugar, mix in the cream cheese and cinnamon. Spread the frosting over the top of the carrot cake using a spatula and decorate with walnut pieces.

Serves 8

Liver Pate

120g bacon
90g butter
225g pig's liver
225g chicken livers
1 onion-sliced
½ tsp salt
¼ tsp pepper
pinch of cayenne pepper
2 tbsp cream

Chop the bacon and fry until fat runs out. Add 30g of the butter and melt. Fry the chopped livers and onion for 5 mins. Mince finely or puree in food processor, add salt, peppers and cream. Place in a buttered terrine or 1½ pint loaf tin, cover with greased paper and then foil. Stand in a roasting tin and half-fill with boiling water. Cook in the oven for 30 mins on 350f 180c gas 4. Middle shelf.
When cooked, remove from water and melt the remaining butter, pour over the surface, allow to cool and leave to set in the fridge, 6 hours.
Serve with hot toast.

Fisherman's Stew

500g selected fish ie; cod, mackerel, salmon
{cut into pieces free from skin and bone}
100g sliced onion
100g leek-chopped
50ml olive oil
1 bayleaf
1 clove garlic
1tbsp chopped parsley
salt and pepper
100ml dry white wine
100g chopped tomatoes-skinned
½ pint fish stock
pinch saffron-if liked

(continued on next page)

Fisherman's Stew (continued)

In a saucepan, fry the onion and leek in oil without colour, add all the fish, bayleaf, chopped garlic, parsley, salt and pepper. Add the wine, tomatoes and stock to cover the fish. Bring to the boil, add saffron-if liked, to add flavour and colour.
Cover with a tight-fitting lid and stew gently for 30 mins.
Serve with sliced french bread.

Serves 4.

Sherry Trifle

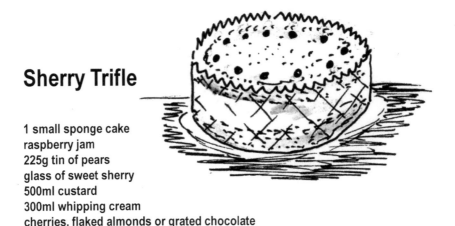

1 small sponge cake
raspberry jam
225g tin of pears
glass of sweet sherry
500ml custard
300ml whipping cream
cherries, flaked almonds or grated chocolate

Cut the sponge into small squares and spread jam on each one.
Place the sponge squares in a bowl or individual glasses.
Drain the fruit, saving the juice and cut them into small pieces, place the fruit over the sponge. Make the sherry up to 150ml with the fruit juice, pour over the sponge and leave to soak. Prepare custard and when nearly cold, spread over sponge and fruit.
Whip the cream until thick, when custard has set pile the cream on top.
Decorate with cherries etc...
Serves 6.

Tomato Soup

450g tomatoes
1 onion
1 carrot
30g butter
30g bacon-chopped
1tbsp tomato puree
1 pint stock
grated nutmeg
squeeze of lemon juice
bunch of herbs
salt and pepper
1tbsp milk
1tsp sugar

Slice the tomatoes, onion and carrot. In a large saucepan, melt the butter and lightly fry the sliced vegetables and bacon for 10 mins. Stir in the tomato puree, add the stock, nutmeg, lemon juice and herbs. Simmer for 45 mins. Liquidize the soup and sieve to remove any skin or pips. Return to the pan, add salt and pepper, a little cold milk and sugar to taste. **Serve hot.**
Serves 4

Beef, roast

Suitable joints for roasting:
Sirloin – 15-20 mins per lb and 15-20 mins extra - 400F 200c gas 6.
Topside or Rolled Rib – 30 mins per lb and 30 mins extra - 375F 190c gas 5.

Weigh the meat to be able to calculate the cooking time. Place joint in a roasting tin, season with salt and pepper, drizzle over a little oil. Put into a very hot oven for 10-15 mins to seal the meat. Then reduce heat to recommended temperature for the joint that you are roasting. Baste with hot fat every 30 mins, when joint is cooked move to another dish, remove string, cover with foil and allow to rest for 15 mins before carving.
Serve with Yorkshire pudding and Horseradish sauce.
(For Thickened Gravy - see week 6).

Yorkshire Pudding

120g plain flour
2 eggs
½ pint milk
salt and pepper

Sieve the flour into a bowl, add the eggs, milk, salt and pepper. Whisk together, pour through a fine sieve and leave to stand for 1 hour at room temperature, stir again before using. Heat the yorkshire pudding tin in the oven with a teaspoon of oil in each well. When smoking hot bring out tray onto a hot surface, fill two-thirds with batter, do this quickly. Bake 25 mins on 425f 210c gas 7. Second shelf from top.
Serve with roast beef.
Serves 6.

Apple Pie

First make the sweet pastry – see week 3
900g apples
120g caster sugar
grated rind of 1 lemon
½ tsp mixed spice
beaten egg

Peel and core the apples, cut them into thick slices. Place apple slices in a bowl and sprinkle over the sugar, lemon rind and mixed spice. Gently mix these ingredients together and leave for 10 mins. Roll out the pastry on a floured surface to 3mm thickness. Grease an oven-proof plate or dish.
Line the plate with the first piece of pastry to form the base, trim the edges. Roll out a second piece for the lid. Arrange neatly the apples on the pasrty plate, brush a little egg around the edge and cover with the second piece for the lid and trim the edges, crimp down with finger-tips to make a pattern and seal by pinching the edges together. Make a small hole in the centre, for the steam to escape. Decorate the top with leaves or shapes cut from the trimmings. Brush over the top with more egg and sprinkle with sugar before cooking. Bake for 40-45 mins on 400f 200c gas 6 until golden.

Serve with a jug of cream.
Serves 6.

Plaice in Breadcrumbs

Ask the fishmonger to fillet and skin four plaice fillets.
Cut each fillet into strips, ½ in wide x 3in long.

Prepare three plates: **1 flour.**
                              2 beaten egg.
                              3 breadcrumbs.

Coat the fish in flour, then into the egg and then breadcrumbs.

Deep fry in vegetable oil until cooked and golden brown, 4-5 mins.
When they float, they are cooked.
Drain onto absorbent paper.
Serve with Tartare sauce and lemon wedges.

Serves 4

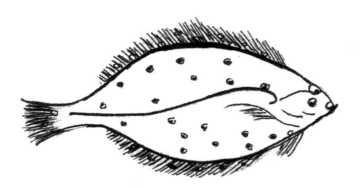

Lancashire Hot Pot

900g lamb-best end of neck
900g potatoes
1 large onion
2 carrots
2 sticks celery
1 leek
salt and pepper
1 tbsp fresh rosemary-chopped
½ pint stock
30g melted butter
extra gravy

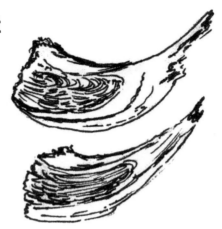

Divide the meat into cutlets, trim off the skin and most of the fat. Peel and slice all the vegetables.Place a layer of potatoes in a greased oven-proof dish. Arrange the cutlets on top and cover with the sliced vegetables, salt, pepper and rosemary. The top layer of potatoes should be smaller and cut in half, arranged to give a neat appearance to the dish. Pour down the side of the dish ½ pint hot stock.
Brush the top layer of potatoes with melted butter and cover with greased paper. Bake for 2 hours on   350f 180c gas 4. After 1½ hours remove the paper to allow the potatoes to become crisp and brown. **Serve with extra gravy. Serves 4**

Jam Omelet

2 eggs-separated
30g caster sugar
a few drops of vanilla essence
15g unsalted butter
1 tbsp warm jam

Beat together the egg yolks, sugar and vanilla essence. Whisk the egg whites until stiff and fold them into the yolks. Heat the butter in a non-stick frying pan, pour in the mixture and cook without stirring over a moderate heat until it just sets. Brown off under a hot grill for a minute. Spread the warm jam in the centre and fold the omelet in half.
Tip out onto a warm plate and dredge with sugar. **Serve at once.**

Serves 2.

Asparagus with Butter

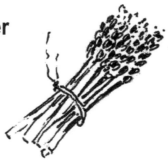

Allow 6 per person
1 bundle of asparagus
pinch of salt
60g butter
squeeze of lemon juice

Trim the hard white ends of the asparagus. Scrape the stalks with a sharp knife, working downwards from the head. Tie them into small bundles of six with the heads all in one direction. Cook very gently in salted boiling water for 5-10 mins. **Serve with melted butter and lemon juice.**

Pork Belly-slow cook

1 belly from a sow, skinned and boned
2 bay leaves
2 tsp coriander seeds
10 white peppercorns
6 cloves
3 star anise
100g salt
150g sugar
1 bunch fresh coriander
4 cloves garlic
1 tsp tabasco sauce

Place all dried spice ingredients in a spice grinder and blitz. Then place salt, sugar, coriander and garlic in a food processor for 3 mins. Add the blitz spices and tabasco to the food processor for a further 2 mins. Rub all over the belly and place in an air-tight container in the fridge for 24 hours.
Rinse well under cold water and pat dry. Wrap twice, first with cling film, second with foil, to make it completely air-tight so no juices can escape, creating a pressure cooker effect.
Place in the oven in a roasting tin and bake for 4 hours on 300f 150c gas 2.
Unwrap and slice as required. **Serves 8.**

Apple Gingerbread

225g cooking apples
30g caster sugar
2 tbsp water

60g soft brown sugar
120g golden syrup
90g butter
175g self-raising flour-sieved
2 tsp ground ginger
1 tsp cinnamon
1 beaten egg

Peel,core and slice the apples, cook with the caster sugar and water until soft, mash to a puree and allow to cool. In a large saucepan, put brown sugar, syrup and butter and melt gently over a low heat. Remove the pan from the heat and stir in the flour, ginger, cinnamon, beaten egg and apple puree.
Grease and line a 7in cake tin with baking parchment paper. Pour the mixture into the tin and bake for 40 mins on 350f 180c gas 4 until golden. Cool on a wire rack, **cut in slices and serve.**

Serves 8

Cheese and Onion Tart

First make short crust pastry – see week 3

Filling: 2 onions
   30g butter
   2 eggs
   ¼ pint double cream
   salt and pepper
   225g cheddar cheese-grated

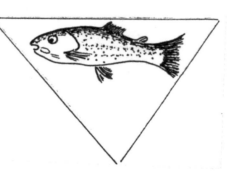

Pre-heat oven to 375f 190c gas 5.
Roll out the pastry on a floured surface to 3mm thickness and line a greased 8in flan case. Peel and slice the onions, fry them in the butter for 15 mins until brown. Place the cooked onions inside the pastry case. Beat the eggs, cream, salt, pepper and grated cheese together. Pour over the onions and bake for 45 mins until set and golden brown.
Serve hot or cold.
Serves 6

Trout Cooked in Foil

1 tsp olive oil
2 rainbow trout fillets
salt and pepper
fresh dill, parsley or thyme
lemon slices and juice

Ask the fishmonger to fillet the fish and remove all bones, giving you two fillets.
Pre-heat oven to 450f 220c gas 8.
Cut squares of foil that are 3 inches longer than your fish. Oil the foil and place the first fillet skin side down, season both sides with salt and pepper.
Place herbs and two slices of lemon down the middle of the fish and place the second fillet on top, skin side up.
Drizzle olive oil over the fish and a good squeeze of lemon juice.
With the fish placed in the middle of the foil-diagonally, fold the square in half to form a triangle shape, folding the edges over twice to make a seal. Place on a metal tray and bake for 15 mins in a hot oven. To serve, place the parcel on a plate and cut across the top to open, remove the fish from the parcel and pour the juices over the top.
Serve with small boiled potatoes.

Rice Pudding with Vanilla

180g short grain or pudding rice
2 pints milk – full fat
60g caster sugar
80g butter
vanilla seeds from 2 pods

Heat the oven to 350f 180c gas 4.
Grease a 2 pint pie-dish. In a saucepan, put the rice, milk, sugar, butter and scraped out vanilla seeds and bring slowly to the boil. Stirring continuously and let it simmer for 5 mins.
Pour the rice mixture into the pie-dish, cover with foil and bake for 50-60 mins until the rice is soft and all the milk has been absorbed. Middle shelf.
Serve with a red fruit jam.

Serves 6

Vegetable Soup

1 onion
1 leek
1 carrot
1 stick of celery
2 large potatoes
1 summer squash
2 pints stock
few sprigs of parsley
salt and pepper

Prepare the vegetables and slice them thinly. Put them all into a large saucepan and cover with the stock. Bring to the boil and simmer for 45 mins until the vegetables are soft. Remove from the heat, add the parsley and liquidize to a puree. Return to the heat, check the seasoning, adding salt and pepper if needed. **Serve piping hot.**
Serves 4

Beef Casserole and Dumplings

450g stewing steak
30g seasoned flour
1tbsp oil
1 onion-sliced
2 carrots-sliced
1 stick celery
60g button mushrooms
½ pint stock
1 tbsp tomato puree
½ pint red wine
½ tsp paprika
¼ tsp nutmeg
salt and pepper

Ask the butcher to dice the beef for you. Toss the beef in the flour that has been seasoned with salt and pepper. In a saucepan heat the oil, fry the onions until golden brown, remove the onions and fry the meat lightly on all sides.
(continued on next page)

Beef Casserole and Dumplings (continued)

Drain and put into a casserole. Next, gently fry the carrots, celery and mushrooms for a few minutes. Add the stock, tomato puree, red wine and seasonings. Bring to the boil, transfer to the casserole. Put the lid on and cook in the oven for 2 hours on 330f 160c gas 3. Middle shelf. After 2 hours, add the dumplings and cook for a futher 20 mins.
Serves 4

For the Dumplings

120g self-raising flour
pinch of salt and pepper
60g vegetable suet
¼ pint water

Sieve the flour, salt and pepper. Stir in suet and water, mix to a slightly soft but not sticky dough.
Divide into eight equal pieces, shape into rounds with lightly floured fingers.
Place on top of the meat and cook for 20 mins.

Apricot Pie

First make the short crust pastry – see week 3
450g fresh apricots-halved and stoned
caster sugar to taste
2 tbsp water
beaten egg

Place the apricots in a 1½ pint pie-dish, sprinkle with sugar and a little water.
Roll out the pastry on a floured surface to 3 mm thickness, a little larger than the pie-dish.
Wet the edge of the dish and place the pastry over the fruit, trim the edges and crimp down to seal.
Decorate as desired, make two slits in the centre for the steam to escape.
Brush with egg, bake for 30-40 mins on 400f 200c gas 6. Sprinkle with sugar, **serve hot or cold.**
Serves 6

Red Windsor and Potato Salad

225g red windsor cheese
2 large potatoes
1 crisp lettuce
1 head of chicory
half a cucumber
3 tomatoes
bunch spring onions
bunch watercress
punnet mustard and cress
2 hard boiled eggs

Peel, dice and cook the potatoes for 15 minutes until just done, drain and allow to cool. Decorate a serving dish with the crisp lettuce and chicory leaves. Thinly slice the cucumber, tomatoes and trim the spring onions. Arrange these on the crisp leaves and garnish with watercress, mustard and cress also cut the hard boiled eggs in half, crumble the cheese over the salad and finish with the cooked potato.
Serve with vinaigrette – see week 22.

Serves 4

For the Vinaigrette
makes ½ pint

240ml extra virgin olive oil
80ml white wine vinegar
pinch of salt
freshly ground black pepper

Whisk the ingredients together, add salt and pepper to taste.

Savoury Rice

2 tbsp vegetable oil
120g bacon-cut into strips
225g long grain rice
1 onion-finely chopped
2 tsp sugar
1 stock cube
225g tomatoes-peeled and chopped
1 pint water
salt and pepper
2 tsp worcestershire sauce
1 small can pineapple pieces
120g cheddar cheese-grated
1 tbsp chopped parsley

In a large saucepan, heat the oil and fry the bacon. Add the rice, onion and gently fry until rice is golden. Remove from heat, add sugar, stock cube, tomatoes, water, salt, pepper and worcestershire sauce. Return to the heat, simmer for 15 mins, until the water has all been absorbed. Stir in the drained pineapple and 60g of the cheese. Serve onto a hot dish, sprinkle over the remaining cheese and parsley. **Serves 4.**

Swiss Roll

120g self-raising flour
pinch of salt
90g butter
90g caster sugar
2 eggs
warm strawberry jam and sugar

Preheat the oven to 425f 210c gas 7. Line a greased tin 9in x 13in x ½ in with baking parchment paper and brush with melted butter. Sieve together the flour and salt. Beat butter and sugar together until light and fluffy, mix in the eggs and flour. Spread evenly into the tin, bake for 10 mins. Third shelf down. Warm the jam in a small pan, have ready a large piece of greaseproof paper dusted with caster sugar. When sponge is cooked, turn out upside down onto sugared paper. Remove tin lining paper quickly, trim off ½ in from edges of sponge. Spread over the warm jam. Starting at the narrow edge nearest you, roll up firmly. Place the join underneath on a wire cooling rack. **Serves 6.**

Fish Cakes

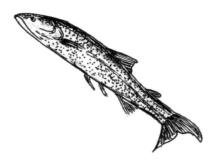

450g mixed cooked fish
30g butter
250g mashed potato
2 eggs
salt and pepper
white breadcrumbs

Remove the skin and bones, then flake the fish. In a saucepan, melt the butter and add the fish, potatoes, yolk of one egg, salt and pepper. Stir over low heat for a few minutes, then turn onto a plate and allow to cool. When cold, shape into round flat cakes, brush over with beaten egg, coat with breadcrumbs and shallow fry in hot oil for 3 mins on each side. Drain onto absorbent paper. **Serves 4**

Chicken, roast

1 roasting chicken about 1.5kg – 2 kg in weight.
4 rashers of bacon
1 tbsp oil
Allow a 1.5 kg chicken to serve 3-4 people.
Allow a 2.5 kg chicken to serve 4-6 people.

Wash and dry thoroughly. Put the chicken into a roasting tin, cover the breast with bacon and a little oil over the top. Roast, for 1 hour on 375f 190c gas 5 until tender, basting several times with hot fat. Remove the bacon 20 mins before the end and roll up to make bacon rolls. Allow breast to brown. Middle shelf. **Serve with sage and onion stuffing.** **For Thickened Gravy – see week 6.**

For the Sage and Onion Stuffing

2 onions
4 fresh sage leaves-chopped
125g breadcrumbs
60g vegetable suet
1 tbsp chopped parsley
grated rind of ½ lemon
¼ tsp salt and a pinch of pepper
1 beaten egg (continued on next page)

Sage and Onion Stuffing (continued)

Peel and slice the onions, boil them for 20 mins in a little water, allow to cool. Mix all the ingredients together and bind to a stiff paste with the egg. With a little flour on your hands, roll into balls. Bake on a greased tray or place around the chicken for 20 mins at 375f 190c gas 5.

Strawberry Cheesecake

For the biscuit base: 250g digestive biscuits
                             120g unsalted butter

Place the biscuits into a plastic bag, crush with a rolling pin into crumbs. In a small pan melt the butter, stir in the biscuit crumbs, until all the butter has been absorbed. Press the mixture into an 8in cake tin with the back of a spoon to form the base. Leave in the fridge to set for 45 mins.

For the filling: **3 leaves gelatine, 500g soft cream cheese**
                       500ml double cream, 150g caster sugar
                       juice of 2 lemons

Place the gelatine in cold water to soak for 10 mins. In a large saucepan, gently warm together the cream cheese, double cream, sugar and lemon juice. Whisking until smooth. Lift out the gelatine and squeeze out any excess water, whisk into the cream mixture until dissolved completely. Remove the biscuit base from the fridge, pour the filling in and allow to cool. Return to the fridge for 3 hours to set.

For the topping: 1 punnet strawberries
                         1 jar apricot glaze

When you are ready to decorate the cheesecake, lift it out of the cake tin and onto a serving plate. Wash the strawberries and remove the stalks, slice and arrange them neatly on the top. Warm the apricot glaze and brush all over the fruit. **Return to the fridge until ready to serve.**

Serves 6-8.

Tomato and Basil Salad

6 large vine plum tomatoes
12 sprigs basil leaves
pinch of salt
freshly ground black pepper
½ pint vinaigrette – see week 22

Wash and dry the tomatoes. Thinly slice the tomatoes lengthways and arrange them neatly in a circle on plates. Place 3 sprigs of basil on each plate and sprinkle over salt and pepper. Make the vinaigrette and use as required.

Serves 4

Baked Lobster

1 cooked lobster – approx 750g – 900g
40g butter
1 shallot-finely chopped
2 tbsp double cream
1 tbsp chopped parsley
juice of ½ lemon
pinch of nutmeg
salt and pepper
1 beaten egg
white breadcrumbs
60g butter-diced

Cut the lobster in half from tail to head, using a sharp knife. Remove the intestinal vein, stomach and gills. Break off the two claws and crack open gently using a wooden mallet. The meat can be removed from the smaller joints of the claws. Remove the lobster meat from the two shells, wash under cold water and clean the two halves, coarsely chop the meat. In a saucepan melt the butter and fry the shallots for 3 minutes without colouring, then add the lobster meat, cream, parsley, lemon juice, nutmeg, salt and pepper to taste. Stir and heat until hot, remove from heat and mix in the egg until it begins to bind. Place the mixture into the clean shells and cover lightly with breadcrumbs. Put a few small pieces of diced butter on top and bake for 12 mins on 350f 180c gas 4 until golden. **Serves 2.**

Strawberry Basket

1 small sponge cake
1 glass sweet sherry or fruit juice
1 family block of vanilla ice cream
300ml whipping cream
12 ice cream wafer biscuits
250g strawberries

Cut the sponge to the same size as the ice cream block. Place the sponge onto a
suitable serving dish and soak with sherry or fruit juice. Place the ice cream block on top
of the sponge.
Whip the cream until thick and pipe a band of cream around the sides of the ice cream.
Stand the wafers over-lapping around the four sides and press them to the block. Pipe
cream on top.
Arrange the strawberries on top of the cream. **Serve at once.**

Serves 6.

Cold Cucumber Soup

1 large cucumber
600ml natural yogurt
2 tbsp tarragon vinegar
2 tbsp caster sugar
pinch of salt
freshly ground black pepper
1 tbsp lemon juice
pinch of paprika
1 tbsp chopped parsley

Wash cucumber and remove the skin. Grate or liquidize the cucumber, add the yogurt, vinegar, sugar, salt and black pepper. Add the lemon juice last. Leave in the fridge to chill. Before serving, stir well and sprinkle each bowl with paprika and parsley.
Serves 4.

Macaroni Mushrooms with Bacon

300g macaroni
30g butter
30g plain flour
1 pint milk-warmed
120g cheddar cheese-grated
salt and pepper
1 tbsp oil
200g mushrooms
4 rashers bacon

Cook the macaroni in slightly salted boiling water for 8-10 mins, drain the macaroni and set aside.
In a saucepan melt the butter, stir in the flour and mix well. Slowly whisk in the milk until it forms a smooth sauce, simmer for 10 mins. Add the cheese keeping some back to sprinkle on top. Season with salt and pepper, mix in the drained macaroni and remove from heat. Heat the oil in a frying pan, clean and cut the mushrooms in half and fry them for 10 mins. Cut the bacon into strips and add to the mushrooms, continue to cook for a futher 5 mins until mushrooms are brown. Add the mushrooms and bacon to the macaroni and pour into a pie-dish, sprinkle with the remaining cheese. Bake for 15 mins on 425f 210c gas 7 until nicely browned. Middle shelf. **Serves 4.**

Hazelnut Crunch Ice Cream

75g hazelnuts-skinned
75g caster sugar
6 egg whites
240g caster sugar
400ml double cream

Preheat the oven to 350f 180c gas 4.
Place hazelnuts on a metal tray and lightly roast them for 5-6 mins, roughly chop into small pieces.
Put the 75g of sugar in a heavy based pan on a medium heat, add the hazelnuts but do not stir, just shake the pan as it starts melting. When the sugar starts to turn a light brown tip it out onto a piece of baking parchment paper and leave to cool. When cool break into small chunks.
Whisk the egg whites until fluffy, rain in the sugar and continue to whisk until it forms soft peaks.
In a separate bowl, whisk the cream until its soft whip stage. Fold the cream gently into the egg whites using a spatula, followed by the hazelnut chunks. Spoon the ice cream into a good plastic container with a tight-fitting lid. **Freeze overnight.**

Serves 6-8.

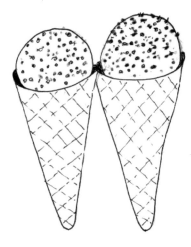

Salmon Mousse

350g fresh salmon steaks
1 egg white
400ml double cream
salt and pepper
1 tbsp chopped dill or parsley
1 tbsp lemon juice

Place the salmon on a metal tray lined with baking parchment paper. Bake in the oven for 15 mins on 375f 190c gas 5, allow to cool once cooked. Once the salmon is cold, remove the skin and scrap off the brown fat by using a small vegetable knife, set aside. Whisk the egg white until stiff.
In a food processor, blend the cooked salmon together with the stiff egg white until smooth.
Add the cream, salt, pepper, chopped herbs and lemon juice, mix again for 10 seconds. Check the taste, spoon into well greased individual moulds or one large mould and cover with foil. Place them in a roasting tin half-filled with boiling water. Put the tin in the oven, middle shelf and bake for 45mins on 310f 150c gas 2. When cooked lift them out of the water to cool, then place in the fridge to set for 6 hours. To turn out, dip each mould into warm water for 5 seconds and onto a serving plate.
Serves 6.

Duck Legs with Red Cabbage

4 duck legs – approx 200g each.
salt and pepper

Wash and dry the duck legs, sprinkle both sides with salt and pepper, Roast for 45 mins on 350f 180 gas 4 until the skin is crispy. Remove from the roasting tin and keep warm. (continued on next page)

For the red cabbage (continued)

1 onion
1 medium size red cabbage
60g butter
1 tbsp malt vinegar
60g brown sugar
1 tbsp cornflour

Finely slice the onion and cabbage. In a large saucepan melt the butter and fry the onion for 5 mins. Add the cabbage, vinegar, sugar and cook for 1 hour with a lid on stirring occasionally. When cooked, mix the cornflour with a little cold water until dissolved, stir into the cabbage to form a syrup that coats the cabbage. Taste for sweetness. To serve, arrange the cabbage on plates and place the duck on top. **Serve with a good gravy.**

Serves 4.

Vanilla Slices

500g puff pastry- ready made
20g cornflour
½ pint milk
2 egg yolks
40g caster sugar
seeds from 1 vanilla pod
icing sugar for dusting

Roll out pasrty on a floured surface to 5mm thickness and cut into fingers 10cm x 3cm. Bake in a hot oven for 12-15 mins on 425f 210c gas 7 until pasrty is well risen and golden, allow to cool on a wire rack. Blend the cornflour with the milk, beat in the egg yolks, sugar and vanilla seeds. Pour the mixture into a heavy based saucepan and cook over a gentle heat until thick, stirring continuously. Allow to cool, to room temperature. Make a slit carefully through the centre of the pastry fingers and cut in half , giving you a top and a base. Neatly spread the custard onto the base and sandwich the two halves together again. Dust the top with icing sugar.
Makes 8 slices.

Haricot Bean and Tomato Soup

175g dried haricot beans
1½ pint stock
225g tomatoes
1 onion
1 carrot
1 potato
30g butter
bunch of herbs
1 bay leaf
pinch of nutmeg
salt and pepper

Wash the beans and soak them in water overnight. Drain and put them in a pan with the stock, bring to the boil and simmer for 1 hour. Meanwhile, slice the tomatoes, onion, carrot and potato. Melt the butter and gently fry the sliced vegetables for 10 mins. Add the fried vegetables to the beans, with the herbs, bay leaf and nutmeg. Simmer until the beans are quite soft. Remove the bay leaf, liquidize the soup until smooth. Reheat, add salt and pepper if needed. **Cooking time – 2 hours.**

Serves 6

Steak Pie

Make the short crust pastry – see week 3
700g lean beef – diced
2 tbsp seasoned flour
2 onions
beef stock
few sprigs of thyme
salt and pepper
1 beaten egg

Ask the butcher to cut the meat into small cubes. Roll the beef through the seasoned flour and place in a casserole with lid, piling them higher in the centre. Peel and finely slice the onions; sprinkle them between the pieces of meat. Sprinkle any remaining flour between the meat. Add enough beef stock to quarter fill the casserole, add the thyme, salt and pepper. Cover with the lid and cook in the oven for 1½ hours on 350f 180c gas 4 until the meat is tender. Middle shelf.

It's a good idea to cook the meat the day before, leaving in the fridge overnight to chill properly. Roll out the pasrty on a floured surface to 3mm thickness, line a greased oven plate with the first piece of pastry. Place the cold meat on top removing the sprigs of thyme. Brush the edges with egg. Roll out a second piece of pasrty and place this over the meat, trim edges and crimp down with fingers to make a seal.

Make a small hole in the centre of the pastry for the steam to escape. Decorate with pastry leaves and brush the top with beaten egg. Bake for 30-35 mins on 375f 190c gas 5 until pastry is golden brown. Second shelf from top.

Serves 6.

Gooseberry Fool

700g gooseberries, 175g caster sugar, ¼ pint water,
2 tbsp custard powder, 3 tbsp sugar, ½ pint milk, ¼ pint double cream

Cook fruit, sugar and water until tender, sieve and cool. Blend custard powder and sugar with a little cold milk, boil remainder. Pour onto custard and return to pan, stir and boil for 3 mins. Cover with damp greaseproof paper to prevent a skin forming. Allow to cool. When both fruit and custard are cold, mix together. Whip up the cream lightly and stir in. Spoon into dessert glasses.

Serves 6

Mushroom and Herb Soup

600g button mushrooms
80g butter
1 onion – sliced
bunch of herbs
2 pints stock
200g potatoes
salt and pepper
dash of cream

Clean the mushrooms. In a large saucepan, melt the butter and fry the onion for 5 mins, add the mushrooms, herbs and stock. Bring to the boil, add the sliced potato, salt, pepper and simmer the soup for 25-30 mins until the potatoes are cooked. Liquidize to a puree, reheat and add the cream.

Serves 6

Sugar Baked Gammon

Choose a piece of gammon, boned and rolled - forehock or collar. Soak for 12 hours. Weigh the joint and calculate the cooking time, allowing 20 mins per lb and 20 mins extra.

For example, a 4lb/1.8kg joint will need 1 hour 40 mins. Place in a large saucepan and cover it with cold water, bring to the boil and simmer for 50 mins. Drain and remove the skin. Score the surface with a knife diagonally to create diamond shapes. Put a whole clove in between each diamond and thickly coat with demerara sugar. Bake for 50 mins on 350f 180c gas 4. Middle shelf. **Serve with pineapple rings, glazed – see week 28.**

Serves 6

Pineapple rings, glazed

8 pineapple rings
2 tbsp brandy
30g melted butter
soft brown sugar

Place pineapple in a shallow oven-proof dish. Pour over brandy and leave to soak for 1 hour. Brush with melted butter, sprinkle with brown sugar. Put under a hot grill to glaze. **Serve around the gammon.**

Cherry Flan

Make sweet pastry – see week 3.
melted chocolate
350g fresh cherries
½ packet raspberry jelly
½ pint hot water

Preheat the oven 400f 200c gas 6.
Roll out pastry on a floured surface to 3mm thickness. Line a greased 8in flan case with the pastry and place on a baking tray. Trim and neaten the edges. Cut a 12in circle of greaseproof paper and place inside the pastry, fill with baking beans and bake for 15 mins. Remove the paper and beans, cook for a further 5 mins to dry the centre. Middle shelf.
When pastry is cold, brush the inside with melted chocolate to create a seal, leave in the fridge to set. Dissolve the jelly in the hot water. Allow to get cold, then put in the fridge until it starts to thicken.
Remove stalks from cherries, cut in half and stone, wash and dry. Arrange cherries in the flan case. When the jelly is starting to thicken, pour over fruit and leave to set in the fridge.

Serves 6

Melon and Smoked Ham

½ ripe honeydew melon
6 thin slices smoked ham
juice of a lemon

Scrap out the seeds. Cut the melon lengthways into six slices. Carefully cut off the skin from each piece, wrap one slice of ham around each melon and squeeze a little lemon juice over each one.

Serves 6

Sea-food Pie

225g cooked white fish
225g cooked smoked haddock
juice of a lemon
2tbsp chopped parsley
2 hard boiled eggs-chopped
¾ pint white sauce
salt and pepper
500g puff pastry-ready made
1 beaten egg

Poach all the fish in a saucepan with enough water to cover for 10 mins. Skin and bone the two fish, break them into large flakes. Mix the fish together, add lemon juice, parsley, eggs and stir in the white sauce. Add salt and pepper to taste. Transfer into a two pint oven-proof dish.
Roll out the pastry on a floured surface to 4mm thickness, slightly bigger than the dish. Cover the dish with the pastry, neatly trim around the edges. Decorate with fish shapes cut from the trimmings. Make a hole in the centre for the steam to escape. Brush with egg and bake for 25 mins on 425f 210c gas 7 until pastry has risen and is golden.

Serves 6

Peach Cheesecake

For the biscuit base:
150g digestive biscuits
100g ginger nut biscuits
120g unsalted butter-melted
350g fresh peaches

For the filling:
500g soft cream cheese
500ml double cream
150g caster sugar
3 leaves gelatine

Place all the biscuits in a plastic bag and crush them with a rolling pin to crumbs. Place the crumbs in a bowl and stir in the melted butter and mix well. Put in an 8in cake tin and press down with the back of a spoon to form the base. Leave in the fridge to set.
Cut the peaches into small pieces, discarding the stones, set aside.
To make the filling, warm together the cream cheese, double cream and sugar {do not allow to boil}.
Place the gelatine in cold water for 5 mins to soften. When soft, squeeze out any excess water and stir into the cream mixture until completely dissolved. Remove from heat and stir in the peach pieces. Pour over the set biscuit base and allow to cool, before returning to the fridge to set. Allow at least 4 hours to set.
Serve with raspberry sauce - see week 29.
Serves 6-8.

Raspberry Sauce

240g fresh raspberries
100g caster sugar
1 tsp lemon juice

Liquidize the raspberries and sugar together until smooth, add lemon juice and strain through a fine sieve to remove any pips. Use as required.
Suitable for all desserts.

Fennel Soup

1 onion
2 leeks
2 celery stalks
1 large fennel bulb
2 potatoes
2 tbsp olive oil
1 pint stock
½ pint milk
salt and pepper
¼ pint cream

Peel and chop all the vegetables. In a large saucepan, heat the oil and gently cook the vegetables for 10 mins with a lid on. Add the stock, bring to the boil and then simmer for 30 mins until the vegetables are tender. Liquidize the soup to a smooth puree, return to the pan and reheat adding the milk. Check the seasoning, add salt and pepper if required. Just before serving, stir in the cream. **Serve hot.**

Serves 4.

Cheese Pie

60g butter
4-6 slices bread
1 tsp mustard
175g cheddar cheese-grated
2 eggs
½ pint milk
salt and pepper
bunch of watercress

Preheat the oven 350f 180c gas 4.
Butter the bread and spread with mustard. Cut each slice into four triangles.
Arrange layers of bread and cheese in a 1½ pint oven-proof dish, finishing with a layer of cheese. Beat together eggs, milk, salt and pepper. Pour over the bread and leave to soak for 30 mins. Bake for 50-60 mins until set. **Serve hot with watercress on the side. Serves 6**

Summer Fruit Mousse

2 egg whites
80g caster sugar
2 leaves gelatine
200ml fruit puree i.e. strawberry, redcurrant, raspberry
480ml double cream

Whisk the egg whites until stiff, add the sugar and continue whisking to soft peaks.
Soak the gelatine in cold water for 5 mins. Slightly warm the puree in a pan.
When the gelatine is soft, squeeze out any excess water and stir into the warm puree
until completely dissolved, allow to cool. In another bowl, whip the cream until slightly
thick. Fold the cream into the meringue, followed by the puree, until well mixed. Pour into
individual glasses or moulds and leave to set in the fridge – **4 hours.**

Serves 6.

Avocado and Olive Tart

First make the short crust pastry – see week 3
2 ripe avocado pears
100g black olives
lemon juice
2 eggs
½ pint milk
salt and pepper

Roll out the pasrty on a floured surface to 3mm thickness. Line either individual pasrty cases or 8in flan cases which have been lightly greased. Cut the avocado in half, and carefully remove the stone. Scoop out the flesh and cut into cubes, sprinkle with lemon juice to prevent turning brown.
Cut the olives in half, remove stones-if any. Beat eggs, milk, salt and pepper together. Place the diced avocado and olives inside the pasrty cases, pour over the egg mixture and bake for 35-40 mins on 350f 180c gas 4 until set.

Makes 8.

Seabass with Cream and Mushroom Sauce

1 tbsp olive oil
4 fillets of seabass approx 175g-200g each
1 shallot-chopped
80g button mushrooms-sliced
100g dry white wine
200ml double cream
salt and pepper

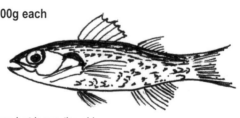

Ask the fishmonger to fillet the seabass but leave the skin on.
Heat the oil in a non-stick frying pan, season the fish on both sides with salt and pepper, place the fish in skin-side down. When the fish is browned turn the fillets over and cook the other side for 5 mins on a low heat. Remove from the pan and keep warm. In the same pan, fry the shallots for 5 mins, add the mushrooms and cook until brown. Add the wine, bring to the boil. Pour in the cream, boil again for 2 mins. Check for taste.
To serve, place the seabass on a nice plate, spoon the mushrooms over the fish and the sauce all around. **Serve with small boiled potatoes and green beans.**
Serves 4.

Plum Cobbler

800g plums
juice and rind of 1 orange
1 cinnamon stick
2 tbsp light brown sugar

For the scone topping:
200g self-raising flour
pinch of salt
1 tsp baking powder
30g unsalted butter-diced
30g caster sugar
100ml milk

Cut the plums in half, remove the stones and place in a 2 pint oven-proof dish. Add the orange juice, rind, cinnamon stick, sugar and mix together.
To make the scone topping: Sieve the flour, salt and baking powder into a bowl.
Rub in the butter until it resembles breadcrumbs, mix in the sugar and make a well in the centre.
Add the milk and mix well to form a firm dough. Roll out on a floured surface to 1cm thickness. Use a 4 cm pastry cutter to cut out the scones, place over the fruit until all is covered. Brush the scones with a little milk, bake for 30 mins on 350f 180c gas 4 until golden. **Serve hot, remember to remove the cinnamon stick.**

Serves 6.

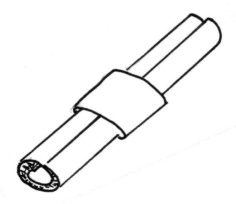

Kipper Pate

2 kippers – boned
1tbsp double cream
100g soft butter
juice of ½ lemon
pinch of cayenne pepper

Place the kippers in a food processor and blend until smooth. Add cream, butter, lemon juice and pepper. Blend again to mix, transfer the pate into a suitable container and store in the fridge. **Serve with hot toast.**

Serves 4.

Venison, saddle

2kg fillet of venison
30g butter
1 carrot
1 onion
1 pint stock
salt and pepper
2 tbsp plain flour
2 tbsp redcurrant jelly
1 glass red wine
¼ pint double cream

Melt the butter in a large casserole and brown the meat all round. Peel and chop the carrot and onion, put in the dish with the stock, add salt and pepper and braise with a tight-fitting lid for 2 hours on 325f 160c gas 3. When cooked remove the meat and vegetables, mix the flour with a little water and stir into the gravy. Let it boil on the hob for 5 mins to slightly thicken. Strain into a clean saucepan and add the redcurrant jelly. Add the wine and simmer for 4 mins, finish with the cream and simmer for 2 mins. Check for taste. **To serve:** Slice the venison and pour the sauce over it. Only small boiled potatoes, carrots and peas necessary with this dish.
Serves 8.

Chocolate Mousse

100g dark chocolate – 70%
25ml black coffee
4 egg whites
20g caster sugar
whipping cream to decorate

Melt the chocolate in a bowl over a pan of simmering water. Stir the coffee into the chocolate once it has melted. In another bowl, whisk the egg whites until stiff, add the sugar and continue whisking until it forms soft peaks. Remove the chocolate from the heat and allow to cool, fold the egg whites into the chocolate, until smooth. Put the mousse into nice glasses and leave in the fridge to set for 4 hours.
Top with whipped cream.

Serves 4.

Apple and Cucumber Salad

1 cucumber
3 dessert apples
salt and pepper
lemon juice
300ml sour cream walnut
pieces-optional fresh
mint-finely chopped

Slice the cucumber thinly. Quarter, core and slice the apples, season with salt and pepper and sprinkle with lemon juice. Stir in the sour cream to bind, add the walnuts and sprinkle with mint.
Serves 6.

Roast Chicken Pie

1 chicken for roasting 1kg-1.5kg
1 onion
1 carrot
30g butter
3 bacon rashers-chopped
1 tbsp chopped parsley
½ pint brown gravy
salt and pepper
500g puff pastry-ready made
1 beaten egg

Roast the chicken for 1½ hours on 375f 190c gas 5. Peel and slice the onion and carrot. In a large saucepan, melt the butter and fry the onion and bacon gently for 5 mins. Add the carrot, parsley, gravy, salt and pepper, simmer for 15 mins, set aside. When the chicken is cooked, remove all meat from the bones and tear into strips. Add meat to the gravy mixture and stir well – should be nice and thick. Transfer into a suitable oven-proof dish. Roll out the pastry to 4mm thickness on a floured surface, slightly large than the dish and place the pasrty over the top to cover the meat, press down around the edges and trim with a knife. Make two holes in the centre for the steam to escape and brush with beaten egg. Lightly score a criss-cross pattern across the top to decorate. Bake for 30-35 mins on 400f 200c gas 6 until golden brown.
Serves 6.

Corn-on-the-Cob

Preparation:
Strip the green husks off the cobs and remove the silky threads.

Cooking methods:
1. Boiling - Cook whole corn cobs in slightly salted boiling water for 8-10 mins.
2. Steaming - Steam for 12-15 mins.

Serve with butter, salt and pepper.

Summer Pudding

900g blackberries, blackcurrants, raspberries or any other soft fruit
225g sugar
½ a loaf of white bread

Cook the fruit and sugar until tender.
Cut the bread into thin slices and remove the crusts.
Line a greased 1½ pint basin with bread, pour in the fruit.
Cover with thin slices of bread. Place a saucer and weight on top. Leave for several
hours or overnight in the fridge. **Turn out and serve with custard or cream.**

Serves 6.

Chilled Spicy Tomato Soup

700g fresh tomatoes
4 slices white bread
2 cloves garlic
1 tbsp red wine vinegar
3 tbsp olive oil
500ml tomato juice
2 sweet red peppers-tinned
1 small onion - finely diced
pinch of salt
½ tsp cayenne pepper
ice cubes

Make the ice cubes the day before. Skin, chop and seed the tomatoes.
Cut the crusts off the bread and crumble it into a bowl. Peel and crush the garlic into the bowl, stir in the vinegar and olive oil. Add the chopped tomatoes, juice, red peppers, onion, salt and cayenne pepper. Liquidize the soup until smooth, leave in the fridge to chill. **To serve: Pour the soup into bowls, place an ice cube in the centre of each soup bowl.**

Serves 6.

Prawns and Cucumber on Skewers

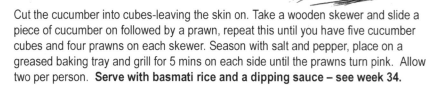

8 wooden skewers
32 large raw shelled prawns
1 large cucumber
salt
black pepper

Cut the cucumber into cubes-leaving the skin on. Take a wooden skewer and slide a piece of cucumber on followed by a prawn, repeat this until you have five cucumber cubes and four prawns on each skewer. Season with salt and pepper, place on a greased baking tray and grill for 5 mins on each side until the prawns turn pink. Allow two per person. **Serve with basmati rice and a dipping sauce – see week 34.**

Serves 4.

For the dipping sauce

½ onion-finely chopped
6 tbsp lime juice
3 tbsp sugar
4 tbsp fish sauce
2 tbsp sesame oil
2 tsp tabasco sauce
1 tbsp fresh coriander- finely chopped
pinch of salt

Place all the ingredients into a bowl, mix together well. Spoon into small dishes and serve on the side.

Blackcurrant and Mint Pie

First make the sweet pastry – see week 3
450g blackcurrants
1 tbsp fresh mint-chopped
125g caster sugar

Top and tail the blackcurrants and wash them well. Drain the blackcurrants and put them in a 8in pie-dish. Mix the finely chopped mint with the sugar and sprinkle it evenly over the fruit.
Roll out the pastry on a floured surface to 4 mm thickness. Cover the pie-dish with the pastry, trim the edges and decorate with pastry leaves cut from the trimmings. Make a hole in the centre for the steam to escape.
Brush the surface with water and sprinkle over a little caster sugar.
Bake for 35-40 mins on 400f 200c gas 6 until golden. **Serve with fresh cream.**

Serves 6.

Crispy Bacon, Lettuce and Celery Salad

8 rashers of streaky bacon
2 baby gem lettuce
1 celery heart
8 cherry tomatoes
1 bunch watercress

Grill the bacon until crispy, drain on absorbent paper. Cut the base off the lettuce and separate all the leaves, wash and dry them well. Arrange the washed leaves in a salad bowl, cut the celery into dice saving the leaves, cut the tomatoes in half. Add the celery, tomatoes and watercress to the lettuce, cut the crispy bacon in half and place on top. Decorate with the celery leaves. **Serve with a simple vinaigrette – see week 22.**

Serves 4.

Hamburgers

500g ground beef – minced
½ onion-finely chopped
1 tbsp flat leaf parsley – chopped
1 egg
1 tbsp tomato ketchup
½ tsp salt
freshly ground black pepper

4 floured baps
iceberg lettuce
tomato
sliced cheese – (optional)

Mix all the ingredients together well. Divide into four, each weighing 165g-175g. Shape into burgers ½in thick, place them on a metal tray and put them under a medium-heat grill for 20 mins, turning halfway. Place a slice of cheese on top, two minutes before the end to melt - if liked. Warm the baps and slice the lettuce and tomato. **To serve:** Place a little lettuce on the bottom half of the bap, sit the burger on the lettuce and arrange more lettuce and sliced tomato on top. Replace the lid, **serve at once with relish or tomato ketchup.**
Serves 4.

Raspberry Trifle

1 punnet fresh raspberries
8 sponge fingers
any fruit juice of choice
500ml custard
300ml whipping cream
pistachio nuts – chopped

Arrange the sponge fingers into glasses. Place raspberries on top.
Pour fruit juice over sponge, enough to soak.
Make the custard quite thick and pour over the sponge and fruit.
Allow to cool, leave in the fridge to set.
Whip the cream until thick and pipe on top, decorate with pistachio nuts.
Can be prepared ahead and left in the fridge until ready to serve.
Setting time 2 hours.

Serves 4.

Butternut Squash Soup

1 large squash
1 onion
1 carrot
1 leek
1 sweet potato
30g butter
1 pint stock
salt and pepper
a little cream

Peel and chop all the vegetables. In a large saucepan melt the butter, fry the onion, carrot and leek for 5 mins. Add the squash and potato, cover with stock and bring to the boil. Simmer for 30 mins until the vegetables are soft. Liquidize the soup to a smooth puree, return to the heat, check for taste adding salt and pepper if required.
Serve hot with a swirl of cream.

Serves 6.

Guinea Fowl – whole roasted

1 guinea fowl, about 1.5kg
50g butter
salt and pepper
3 slices streaky bacon

Wash the bird inside and out. Mix the butter with salt and pepper, place inside the body of the bird.
Lay the slices of bacon over the breasts and roast for 1¼ hours on 375f 190c gas 5.
Carve the same as chicken. **Serve with lemon and thyme stuffing – see week 36.**
For Thickened Gravy – see week 6.

Serves 4.

Lemon and Thyme Stuffing

1 onion
1 tbsp fresh thyme leaves
125g breadcrumbs
60g suet
grated rind and juice of 1 lemon
¼tsp salt
pinch of pepper
1 egg

Finely dice the onion, mix all the ingredients together to form a firm paste.
Place into a greased oven-proof dish and bake for 30 mins on 400f 200c gas 6.

Serves 4.

Pear and Blackberry Crumble

700g pears
100g caster sugar
rind and juice of ½ lemon
200g blackberries

Crumble topping:
200g plain flour
100g butter
100g sugar
½ tsp mixed spice
brown sugar

Peel, core and quarter the pears.
Place in a pan with the sugar and ¼ pint water, lemon rind and juice.
Cook gently for 10 mins with a lid on until soft.
Place in a 2 pint oven-proof dish, put the blackberries on top of the pears.
Sift the flour, rub in the butter to resemble breadcrumbs, add the sugar and mixed spice.
Sprinkle the crumble over the fruit and finish with a little brown sugar on top.
Bake for 30 mins on 350f 180c gas 4 until golden. **Serve with custard or fresh cream.**

Serves 6.

Game Soup

chopped carcases and trimmings
of 2 partridges or pheasants
30g lean bacon-chopped
30g butter
1 onion. 1 carrot. ½ parsnip. 1 stick of celery
30g flour
2 pints stock
seasonal herbs. 1 clove
some neat pieces of breast of bird
salt and pepper

Put the carcase pieces, trimmings and bacon, with the butter in a saucepan and fry them until brown. Remove the bones and meat and fry the sliced vegetables until brown. Add the flour and mix in well. Stir in the stock and bring to the boil, add the herbs, clove and return the bones etc.. to the pan and simmer for 1½ hours. Cut the pieces of breast meat into ¼in dice. Strain the soup, reheat adding the diced breast. Add salt and pepper if required. **Serves 6.**

Fish Pie with Cheesy Mash

400g mixed raw fish
salt and pepper
lemon juice. 1 tbsp chopped parsley
½ pint white sauce
1 hard boiled egg

For the cheesy mash
450g potatoes. 20g butter. a little milk
100g cheddar cheese-grated

Grease a 2 pint oven-proof dish.
Boil the potatoes, chop the parsley, make the white sauce and hard boil the egg for 7 minutes. Cut the raw fish into large cubes. Peel and quarter the egg. Mix the fish into the sauce, add salt, pepper, lemon juice and parsley. Add the egg quarters. Drain, dry and mash the potatoes, add salt, pepper, butter, milk and cheese to make a creamy mash. Put the fish mixture into the dish and cover with the mashed potato, smooth it over with a fork. Bake for 45mins on 400f 200c gas 6 until the top is golden brown. **Serves 4.**

Apple Mousse

675g apples
180ml milk
3 eggs-separated
75g caster sugar
2 tsp lemon juice
150ml double cream-whipped
15g sachet of gelatine
4 tbsp water
few drops of green food colouring
whipped cream to decorate

Peel, core and chop the apples. Cook them in 2 tbsp water until soft, liquidize to a smooth puree and leave to cool. Heat the milk gently, beat the egg yolks and sugar together until thick, stir in the milk and return the mixture back to the pan and cook over a low heat, until thick custard. Cool.

Put the apple puree into a large bowl, stir custard and lemon juice into the apple, then fold in the whipped cream. Dissolve the gelatine in water, using its own instructions and stir into the apple mixture. Chill. When the mixture is just starting to set, whisk the egg whites until stiff and fold into the mixture, with a little green colouring. Pour into wetted 2 pint mould or individual glasses, leave in the fridge to set.

Decorate with whipped cream. Served chilled.

Serves 6.

Broccoli and Stilton Soup

600g broccoli spears
30g butter
1 onion-sliced
1 stick celery-sliced
2 pints vegetable stock
200g potatoes-sliced
salt and pepper
100g blue stilton cheese
dash of cream

Trim the broccoli and cut into small pieces. In a large saucepan melt the butter and fry the onion and celery for 5 mins. Add the broccoli, stock, potatoes and cook for 30 mins until the vegetables are soft. Liquidize to a smooth puree. Return to the pan and reheat, crumble the stilton and stir in, but do not allow to boil. Add salt and pepper if required. **Serve hot with a dash of cream.**

Serves 6.

Grandmother's Gratin

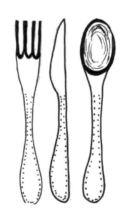

450g smoked haddock-skinned
150ml milk
pinch of pepper
30g butter
2 hard-boiled eggs, chopped
90g cheddar cheese-grated
30g breadcrumbs

Place haddock in a 2 pint oven-proof dish. Cover with milk, pepper and butter. Bake for 15 mins on 350f 180c gas 4 until fish is cooked. Mix together the eggs, cheese and breadcrumbs. Sprinkle over the fish and return to the oven for 20-25 mins to brown. **Serve hot.**

Serves 4.

Pumpkin Pie

First make the sweet pasrty – see week 3.
450g pumpkin puree
140g sugar
½ tsp salt and freshly ground black pepper
½tsp grated nutmeg. ½tsp cinnamon. ¼tsp ground cloves.
4 whole eggs
175ml double cream
icing sugar to decorate

Roll out the pasrty on a floured surface to 3mm thickness. Line a greased 8in flan case, trim the edges.
Place a circle of greaseproof paper inside the pastry case and fill with baking beans.
Bake for 15mins on 400f 200c gas 6. Middle shelf.
Remove the beans and paper, return to the oven for a further 3-5 mins to dry the centre.

For the filling:
Cut the pumpkin in half and scoop out the seeds, cut away the skin with a sharp knife.
Cut the pumpkin flesh into large cubes and wrap in foil, place on a baking tray.
Bake in the oven for 45 mins on 400f 200c gas 6 until cooked. Remove the foil, allow to cool. In a large bowl, mix the sugar, salt, pepper, spices, eggs and cream together.
Liquidize the cooked pumpkin to a puree. Stir the puree into the egg/cream mixture and mix in well. Pour this into the cooked pasrty case and bake for 45 mins on 350f 180c gas 4 until set. Middle shelf. Allow to cool, dust with icing sugar and cut into portions.

Serves 6.

Stuffed Flat Mushrooms

4 large flat mushrooms
4 tbsp sunflower oil
60g butter
salt and pepper
1 onion. 1 courgette. 1 red pepper. 2 baby leeks.
2 cloves garlic
sprig of fresh rosemary
100g cheddar cheese-grated

Clean the mushrooms and remove the centre stalks. Place on a baking tray, sprinkle each one with oil and pieces of butter, salt, pepper and cover with foil. Cook in an oven for 20mins on 400f 200c gas 6. Meanwhile, prepare and cut all the vegetables into small dice, including the mushroom stalks.

In a frying pan, cook the vegetables in oil with the garlic and rosemary for 10mins. When the mushrooms are cooked remove the foil, fill each one with the cooked vegetables. Top with grated cheese and return to the oven for 10 mins, until golden brown. Middle shelf. **Serve with salad leaves.**

Serves 4.

Plaice fried, with Parsley Butter

4 x 125g fillets of plaice
1 tbsp flour
salt and pepper
1 tbsp milk, beaten egg and breadcrumbs
vegetable oil for frying
60g butter. 1 tbsp chopped parsley
lemon wedges

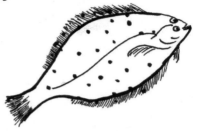

Ask the fishmonger to fillet and skin the fish. Season the flour with salt and pepper, roll each fillet through the flour. Beat the milk and egg together, dip the fish into the egg, then the breadcrumbs. In a frying pan, heat the oil and fry the fish until nicely browned on both sides. **Serve with melted butter, chopped parsley and lemon wedges.**

Serves 4.

Peach and Almond Tart

First make the sweet pastry – see week 3.
120g butter
120g icing sugar
2 eggs
120g ground almonds
15g plain flour
6 ripe peaches
1 small jar apricot glaze

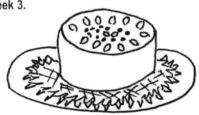

Roll out the pasrty on a floured surface to 3mm thickness. Line a greased 9in flan case, trim around the edges. Beat the butter and sugar together, until thick and white. Add the eggs, ground almonds and flour, mix well. Place the mixture into the pastry case and smooth over with the back of a spoon.
Cut the peaches into quarters and remove the stones. Arrange the quarters, skin side up around the case, pushing them into the almond mixture so just the skin is showing.
Place them 1cm apart and bake for 45-50 mins on 350f 180c gas 4 until golden. Middle shelf. When cooled, brush the top with warm apricot glaze.

Serves 6.

Spiced Autumn Soup

1 onion. 1 leek. 2 carrots. 1 parsnip
1 sweet potato. 1 large potato
2 pints vegetable stock
1 tbsp tomato puree
1 bay leaf. 6 basil leaves
2 red chillies
salt and black pepper

Peel and slice all the vegetables. Place them all in a large saucepan and cover with the stock. Bring to the boil, add the tomato puree, bay leaf, basil leaves and chopped chillies. Simmer for 45mins until the vegetables are soft. Add salt and pepper if required. Remove the bay leaf. Liquidize to a smooth puree.
Serve with crunchy croutons – see week 7.

Serves 6.

Lamb Cutlets in Breadcrumbs

6 lamb cutlets from best end of neck
salt and pepper
1 beaten egg
white breadcrumbs
small boiled potatoes
2 tomatoes for grilling
120g green peas
6og butter. 1 tbsp oil
½ pint gravy

Ask the butcher to trim the cutlets for you. Season both sides with salt and pepper, brush egg over each one, then coat in breadcrumbs. Peel and boil the potatoes, cut the tomatoes in half and grill, boil the peas. In a frying pan, heat the butter with the oil and gently fry the cutlets on both sides until brown, the lamb should be slightly pink in the centre. Finally make the gravy. Arrange the potatoes, peas and grilled tomatoes on a plate and place the cutlets on top. **Serve the gravy in a jug.**

Serves 2.

Beresford Pudding

125g self-raising flour
pinch of salt
125g butter
125g caster sugar
2 eggs
1 tbsp milk
30g breadcrumbs
grated rind and juice of 1½ oranges

Sieve the flour and salt together. Beat the butter and sugar until light and fluffy.
Mix in the eggs, milk, breadcrumbs, rind and juice. Fold in the flour.
Put into a greased 2 pint basin, cover with greaseproof paper and foil, tied around with
string and steam for 1½ hours in a deep saucepan with water in the bottom and a lid on.
When cooked, turn out and serve with orange sauce – see week 40.

Serves 6.

Orange Sauce

2 tsp cornflour
300ml water
juice of ½ a lemon
juice and rind of ½ an orange
30g caster sugar

Blend the cornflour with a little cold water.
Boil the remaining water together with the juices and rind.
Whisk in the blended cornflour, reboil for 2 mins, add the sugar and serve.

Apple and Parsnip Soup

500g apples
1 onion
500g parsnips
1 pint stock
½ tsp mild curry powder
salt and pepper
dash of cream

Peel and core the apples. Peel and chop the onion and parsnips.
Boil the stock, add the apples, onion, parsnips and curry powder. Bring back to the boil, simmer for 40 mins until vegetables are soft. Liquidize to a smooth puree, add a pinch of salt and pepper. **Reheat and serve with a dash of cream.**

Serves 4.

Pheasant Casserole

2 small pheasants – cleaned
30g butter
120g bacon-diced
2 small onions and 1 carrot-sliced
60g plain flour
1 pint stock
salt and pepper
125g button mushrooms
1 tbsp chopped parsley

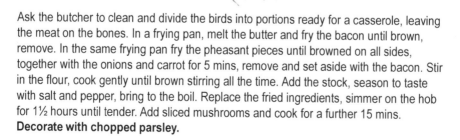

Ask the butcher to clean and divide the birds into portions ready for a casserole, leaving the meat on the bones. In a frying pan, melt the butter and fry the bacon until brown, remove. In the same frying pan fry the pheasant pieces until browned on all sides, together with the onions and carrot for 5 mins, remove and set aside with the bacon. Stir in the flour, cook gently until brown stirring all the time. Add the stock, season to taste with salt and pepper, bring to the boil. Replace the fried ingredients, simmer on the hob for 1½ hours until tender. Add sliced mushrooms and cook for a further 15 mins. **Decorate with chopped parsley.**

Serves 4.

Hot Chocolate Pudding

160g dark chocolate-chopped
125g butter
4 eggs
160g caster sugar
125g self-raising flour
30g cocoa powder

Put the chocolate and butter in a metal bowl, place over a saucepan of simmering water until melted, allow to cool slightly. Meanwhile, beat the eggs and sugar together until light and fluffy.
Mix in the sifted flour and cocoa powder, followed by the melted chocolate. Pour into a baking tin lined with parchment paper and bake for 45-50 mins on 375f 190c gas 5 until firm to touch. **Serve with chocolate fudge sauce – see week 41.**

Serves 6.

Chocolate Fudge Sauce

100g butter
175g dark soft brown sugar
375ml double cream
100g dark chocolate

In a saucepan, melt the butter with the sugar, stirring until almost boiling.
Add the cream, bring to the boil and simmer for 5 mins.
Remove from the heat and allow to cool. When cooled, stir in the chocolate until melted.
Keep warm, serve with hot chocolate pudding.
Do not reboil the sauce.

Chicken Livers and Bacon Salad

500g chicken livers
salt and pepper
8 rashers streaky bacon
4 slices white bread
150g butter
2 tbsp vegetable oil
170ml sherry
mixed salad leaves
vinaigrette – see week 22

Rinse the chicken livers, cut away the white stringy pieces and gall bladder. Season with salt and pepper. Grill the bacon until crispy, place on absorbent paper to dry. Remove the crusts from the bread and cut into 1cm cubes. Melt 100g of the butter in a frying pan together with the oil. When hot, fry the cubes of bread turning them until golden all over, drain on paper. Melt the remaining butter in the same pan and fry the livers for 4 mins on each side, they should be pink in the middle.
Stir in the sherry and simmer until its a syrupy consistency. Wash and dry the salad leaves. **To serve:** Arrange the salad leaves on a plate, place livers around the salad. Sprinkle croutons and top with bacon. **Serve at once with vinaigrette.**

Serves 4.

Cod Steaks, grilled

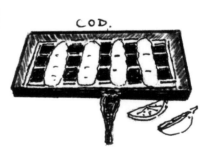

COD.

4 cod steaks – boned
salt and pepper
30g flour
melted butter or oil
white breadcrumbs
lemon wedges

Wash the fish, toss in seasoned flour, brush with melted butter. Grill for 5 mins, turn over and brush with butter, grill for a further 5 mins until cooked. Sprinkle with breadcrumbs and put back under the grill until golden, brushing more butter on top.
Serve with lemon wedges and parsley butter – see week 42.

Parsley Butter

125g butter
2 tbsp chopped parsley
2 tsp lemon juice
freshly ground black pepper

Using soft butter, beat in parsley, lemon juice and black pepper.
Form into a long roll in greaseproof paper and leave in the fridge to harden.
When required, cut off 5mm thick slices.

Bakewell Tart

First make the sweet pastry – see week 3
raspberry jam
lemon curd
120g butter
120g caster sugar
2 eggs
120g ground almonds
15g plain flour
flaked almonds
icing sugar for dusting

Roll out the pastry on a floured surface to 3mm thickness.
Line a 8in flan case with the pastry and neatly trim around the edges.
Spread a good layer of raspberry jam on the bottom, followed by a layer of lemon curd on top of the jam. Cream together the butter and sugar, until thick and white. Beat in the eggs, ground almonds and flour. Spread the mixture over the jam.
Bake for 10 mins, them remove from oven and sprinkle the flaked almonds on top.
Return to the oven and bake for a further 30 mins on 380f 190c gas 5. Middle shelf.
When cooked, remove from case and allow to cool on a wire rack. Dust with icing sugar.
Serve hot or cold.

Serves 6.

Cream of Cauliflower Soup

1 large cauliflower
1 onion
1 stick of celery
30g butter
30g flour
1 pint stock
½ pint milk
few sprigs of parsley
salt and white pepper
dash of cream

Cut away the green stalks and cut the cauliflower into florets. Slice the onion and celery. In a large saucepan, melt the butter and gently cook the onion and celery for 10 mins. Mix in the flour and slowly stir in the stock and the milk. Bring to the boil, add the cauliflower, parsley, salt and pepper.
Simmer for 25 mins until soft, liquidize to a smooth puree and return to the heat.
Add a dash of cream before serving, serve hot.
Serves 4.

Pork Chops with Cider Gravy

4 pork chops
1 clove garlic
1 tbsp olive oil
30g butter
1 onion-sliced
½ pint of cider
½ pint of gravy
few sprigs of thyme
salt and pepper

Peel and crush the garlic and rub this into both sides of each chop. Brush the chops all over with oil and cook them under a hot grill, for 8 mins on each side. Brush the chops again with oil when they are turned. Melt the butter in a small pan, cook the onion for 10 mins. Pour in the cider and cook for 5 mins. Stir in the gravy, add the thyme and simmer for a further 10 mins. Add salt and pepper if required. Pour the gravy over the chops.
Serves 4.

Chocolate and Chestnut Cake
{no baking required}

200g dark chocolate – 70%
100ml water
50g caster sugar
200g chestnut puree
150g unsalted butter-soft
300ml whipping cream
2 tbsp dark rum
cocoa powder for dusting

Melt the chocolate in a metal bowl, over a saucepan of simmering water.
Boil the water and sugar together in a small pan for 2 mins to make a syrup, allow to cool.
Beat the chestnut puree and butter together.
Whip the cream until thick.
Whisk the syrup into the melted chocolate, add the puree mixture and mix in well. Allow to cool.
When cooled, fold in the cream and rum using a spatula.
Spoon the mixture into a 9in round tin, lined with cling film, cover the top with cling film too.
Leave in the fridge for at least 6 hours to firm. Cut and serve straight from the fridge.
Dust each serving with cocoa powder, serve with whipped cream.

Serves 8-10.

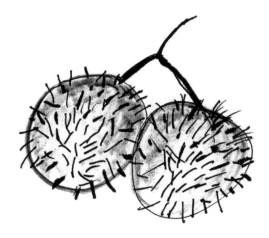

Pumpkin Soup

1 small pumpkin
2 leeks
2 potatoes
50g butter
2 pints stock
salt and pepper

Cut the pumpkin in half, clean out the seeds and cut away the skin with a sharp knife. Cut the flesh into large cubes. Wash and finely chop the leeks, peel and roughly chop the potatoes.

In a large saucepan, melt the butter and cook the leeks until soft. Add the pumpkin, potato and stock.

Bring to the boil, simmer for 45 mins until potatoes are soft. Liquidize the soup to a smooth puree, add salt and pepper if required. **Serve hot.**
Serves 6.

Toffee Apples

12 eating apples
450g granulated sugar
1 tsp cream of tartar
1 tsp honey
300ml water

Wipe the apples clean with a cloth and stick a wooden skewer in each one. Grease a baking tray. Put sugar, cream of tartar, honey and water into a thick based saucepan. Allow sugar to dissolve over a gentle heat. Then boil until mixture is light caramel in colour {315f on sugar thermometer} or the hard crack stage. This will take about 20 mins. Dip each apple into the caramel and coat it completely, then place on the greased baking sheet to harden.

Pizza

For the dough:
225g plain flour, 1 tsp salt, 15g yeast
approx 150ml lukewarm milk
1 egg-small
30g butter, soft

Sieve the flour and salt. Cream yeast with a little warm milk, beat the egg and add with the rest of milk to the yeast. Add liquid gradually to flour, add softened butter. Knead well with the hand until mixture comes away from the fingers. Cover with a cloth, leave for 40 mins in a warm place.

For the filling:
1 tbsp oil
1 small onion-chopped
225g tin tomatoes
60g tomato puree
1 tsp sugar
salt and pepper

1 tin tuna fish
50g cheese-grated
small tin anchovy fillets
black olives-stoned
1 bay leaf

Method for pizza: Heat the oil and fry the onion until tender and golden. Add the tomatoes, puree, sugar, salt, pepper and bay leaf. Simmer for 20 mins, cool, add drained tuna. Grease a large baking tray, pat out dough with the hands to a round about 9in in diameter. Cover to within ½in of the edge with filling. Decorate with anchovies, cheese and olives. Leave pizza in a warm place for 20 mins. Bake for 25-30 mins on 425f 210c gas 7. Middle shelf. **Serves 6.**

Witch's Brew

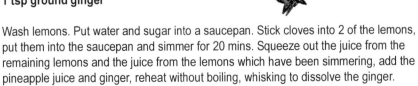

6 lemons, 2 pints water
175g demerara sugar,12 cloves
2 pints pineapple juice
1 tsp ground ginger

Wash lemons. Put water and sugar into a saucepan. Stick cloves into 2 of the lemons, put them into the saucepan and simmer for 20 mins. Squeeze out the juice from the remaining lemons and the juice from the lemons which have been simmering, add the pineapple juice and ginger, reheat without boiling, whisking to dissolve the ginger.
Serves 10 glasses.

Game Pate

300g streaky bacon
2 pheasant breasts-diced
700g belly pork-minced
300g mixed game meat-diced
2 tbsp fresh thyme leaves
2 tbsp chopped parsley
salt and freshly ground black pepper
150ml red wine
1 tbsp brandy

Ask the butcher to mince the belly pork, dice the game and pheasant for you.
Line a 2 pint loaf tin with bacon, saving some to cover the top.
In a bowl, put the belly pork, diced meat, herbs, salt and pepper. Pour in the red wine and brandy, mix well and put into the lined tin. Place bacon over the top, cover with greaseproof paper and foil.
Place the pate in a roasting tin and half fill the tray with boiling water, cook in the oven for 2 hours on 300f 150c gas 2. Middle shelf. When cooked, lift the pate out of the water, allow to cool then leave in the fridge overnight. Run a small knife around the edge of the pate to remove from tin.
To serve: Slice the pate, serve with hot toast and salad.

Serves 10-12.

Goose, roast
Goose (3.5-4kg dressed weight)

Parsley and Orange Stuffing

1 small brown loaf
3 rashers bacon-chopped
75g butter
2 tbsp chopped parsley
salt and pepper
juice of 2 oranges
1 egg

Method for stuffing.
Remove the crusts from the loaf and grate into breadcrumbs.
Dice the bacon and fry in its own fat.
Rub butter into the crumbs, add bacon, parsley, salt and pepper. Bind together with orange juice and egg. Use to stuff neck end of the goose.
Wrap the bird in foil. Roast for 4½ hours, unwrapping foil for the last ½ hour to brown skin, {baste}. Cook on 330f 160c gas 3. Middle shelf.
When goose is cooked remove the string and allow to rest before carving.
To make Thickened gravy – see week 6.

Jam Tarts

First make short crust pastry – see week 3.
Strawberry jam or jam of your choice

Roll out the pastry on a floured surface to 3mm thickness.
Use a 8cm pastry cutter to cut out circles of pastry.
Place each one in a greased shallow yorkshire pudding tray, that makes 12.
Press down to create the shape.
Half fill each case with jam and bake for 10-15 mins on 425f 210c gas 7.
Allow to cool, before serving.

Potted Prawns

300g butter
freshly grated nutmeg
pinch of salt and cayenne pepper
450g cooked and peeled prawns

In a saucepan, melt 200g of the butter with the nutmeg, salt and cayenne pepper.
Remove from the heat and cool slightly, add the prawns and spoon into six small pots.
Melt the remaining butter on a low heat, spoon the clear butter over the prawns.
Leave in the fridge to set for 3 hours. Remove pots 30 mins before serving, to come to
room temperature. **Serve with hot toast and lemon wedges.**

Serves 6.

Steak and Kidney Pudding

700g stewing steak-diced
150g ox kidney-diced
1 onion
2 tbsp flour
salt and pepper
(continued on next page)

For the suet crust pastry: (continued)

250g self-raising flour, 125g suet, pinch of salt, water to bind
In a bowl, mix the flour, suet and salt together. Use enough water to form a dough.

Ask the butcher to cut the steak and kidneys into ½in dice. Peel and thinly slice the onion. Roll the steak and kidney in the seasoned flour and mix in the onion.
Make the suet crust pastry. Set aside a quarter for the lid. Roll out the remainder to a circle ½in thickness. Grease a 1½ pint pudding bowl and line with the pastry, to the bottom and sides. Spoon in the meat and onion and fill two-thirds with cold water. Roll out the remaining pastry to a circle to fit the top. Dampen the edges with water and fit the lid tightly to seal, trim off excess pastry.
Tie a piece of double thickness greaseproof paper, over the top of the bowl. Wrap the string around twice and tie tightly. Place the bowl in a deep saucepan and pour boiling water half way up the sides. Gently boil for 4 hours, topping up the water if it gets too low. **Serve with small boiled potatoes, brussel sprouts and extra gravy.**
Serves 4.

Apple Crumble

700g apples
125g caster sugar
grated rind of ½ lemon
100ml water

For the crumble:
175g plain flour
75g butter
60g caster sugar
½ tsp mixed spice
brown sugar to sprinkle on top

Peel, quarter and core the apples into a pan. Add the sugar, lemon rind and water, cook gently with a lid on until soft. Put the apples into a 2 pint oven-proof dish. Allow to cool.
For the crumble: Rub the butter into the flour until it resembles breadcrumbs, add the caster sugar, mixed spice and mix in well. Sprinkle the crumble over the apples and spread out evenly. Bake for 40 mins on 350f 180c gas 4 until golden. Middle shelf.
Serve with custard or fresh cream.
Serves 6.

Carrot and Leek Soup

250g carrots
250g leeks
1 onion, 1 potato
30g butter
1½ pints stock
1 bay leaf
salt and pepper

Peel and slice the vegetables. In a saucepan, melt the butter and gently cook the vegetables for 10 mins with a lid on, stirring from time to time. Add the stock, bay leaf and simmer for 30 mins until the vegetables are soft. Remove the bay leaf and liqiudize the soup to a smooth puree. Add salt and pepper if required. **Serve hot.**
Serves 6.

Liver and Bacon

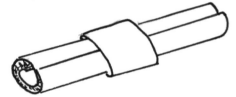

500g lambs liver
250g rashers of bacon
seasoned flour
1 onion-sliced
30g butter
450ml stock

Wash the liver in cold water and remove any tubes or blood vessels.
Dry the liver and cut into ½in thick slices. Dip each slice into seasoned flour. Fry the bacon, set aside. Fry the liver in the fat from the bacon, quickly on each side. Remove from the pan and put the liver in a warm place with the bacon on top. Fry the onion in the butter for 5 mins, add a little flour to the fat and stir in until browned. Stir in the stock to make the gravy, place the liver and bacon back in the gravy and simmer for 15 mins. Season to taste. **Serve with parsnip mash – see week 47. Serves 6.**

Parsnip mash

500g potatoes, 2 large parsnips, 30g butter, salt and pepper

Peel and cut the vegetables into large dice. In a saucepan, boil the potato and parsnip together in slightly salted water for 30 mins until soft. Drain and let dry. Mash well. Add the butter, salt and pepper to taste. **Serve hot with the main course.**

Sticky Toffee Pudding

280g chopped dates
520ml water
20g bicarbonate of soda
Bring these ingredients to the boil, drain, allow to cool.

280g butter
420g soft dark brown sugar
6 eggs
420g plain flour
30g baking powder

Beat together the butter and sugar. Sift the flour with the baking powder.
Add the eggs one at a time, adding a spoonful of flour with each egg, until all the flour is
mixed in. Stir in the drained dates thoroughly. Line a baking tray 12x10in with baking
parchment paper, pour the mixture in. Bake for 40 mins on 350f 180c gas 4 until the
sponge is firm and springy. Middle shelf. Cut into squares, **serve with toffee sauce -
see week 47.** {vanilla ice cream goes very well with this dessert}.

Serves 12.

Toffee Sauce

250g butter
375g soft dark brown sugar
550ml double cream

In a thick based saucepan, melt the butter and sugar together and bring to the boil.
Stir in the cream, reboil again and simmer for 5 mins. **Serve hot with sticky toffee
pudding.**

Scotch Broth

500g neck of mutton
4 pints stock
60g barley
2 carrots
2 turnips
1 onion
salt and pepper
1 tbsp chopped parsley

Cut the meat into small pieces. In a large saucepan, bring the mutton and stock to the boil. Add the barley, sliced vegetables, salt and pepper. Reboil, then simmer for 2 hours. Remove the meat from the bones and cut up if necessary. Season to taste. **Serve hot. Sprinkle with chopped parsley just before serving**

Serves 8.

Minced Beef and Thyme Dumplings

500g ground minced beef
2 onions
1 tbsp oil for frying
pinch of salt and pepper
1 pint stock

For the Dumplings see week 21
Mix in 1 tbsp fresh thyme leaves.

Peel and finely chop the onions. In a large saucepan, heat the oil and fry the onions for 5 mins until soft. Add the minced beef and fry until browned and has separated. Add salt and pepper and pour in the stock, until meat is almost covered. Simmer for 50 mins, with the lid on stirring occasionally.
After 30 mins, put the dumplings on top of the minced beef and continue cooking for a further 20 mins, replace the lid. **Serve two dumplings per person.**

Serves 4.

Cranachan
(Traditional Scottish Dessert)

55g pinhead oatmeal
300g raspberries-can be frozen
600ml whipping cream
2 tbsp runny honey
3 tbsp malt whisky

Toast the oatmeal, until golden brown. Allow to cool.
Whisk the cream until soft whip stage, add the honey and whisky and mix in well.
Set aside some raspberries for decoration.
In individual glasses, start to build up layers of raspberries, cream, toasted oatmeal.
Repeat this all the way up to the top of the glass, decorate with more oatmeal and
raspberries. **Keep in the fridge, until ready to serve.**

Serves 4.

Swede and Nutmeg Soup

500g swede
1 onion
1 carrot
1 potato
30g butter
1 pint stock
1 level tsp nutmeg
1 bay leaf
salt and pepper
dash of cream

Peel and slice all the vegetables. In a large saucepan melt the butter, gently cook the onion for 5 mins.
Adding next the rest of the vegetables, followed by the stock, nutmeg and bay leaf. Bring to the boil, simmer the soup for 30 mins until the vegetables are soft. Remove the bay leaf. Liquidize the soup to a smooth puree, reheat adding salt and pepper to taste.
Put a dash of cream in each soup bowl before serving.

Serves 4-6.

Kippers, grilled

1-2 kippers per person
butter
lemon wedges

Remove the heads and lay the kippers flat, skin side up on a tray. Place under a grill, medium heat for 3 mins on each side, adding a little butter when they are turned over. When the fish is cooked, it should be possible to lift out the bone, starting from the head end. **Serve with brown bread and butter, lemon wedges.**

Poor Knights of Windsor

3 slices of white bread, cut ½in thick
150ml milk
1 tsp caster sugar
½ tsp ground cinnamon
1 egg-beaten
oil for frying
hot jam to sandwich the bread
caster sugar and cinnamon

Cut the bread into fingers, remove the crusts.
Add the sugar and cinnamon to the milk and soak the bread in it, then drain thoroughly.
Beat the egg and turn it onto a plate. Prepare some kitchen paper with caster sugar and
cinnamon. Heat the oil in a frying pan. Dip the bread into the egg, both sides and fry in
the hot oil, one piece at a time. Fry the bread until it is golden brown, turn it over and
brown the other side. Drain on absorbent paper, toss the bread in sugar and cinnamon.
Sandwich two fingers with hot jam. **Serve hot.**

Mince Pies

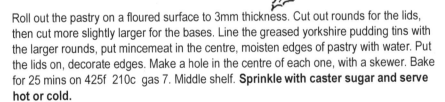

First make the short crust pastry – see week 3.
2 tbsp water. Caster sugar. Mincemeat.

Roll out the pastry on a floured surface to 3mm thickness. Cut out rounds for the lids,
then cut more slightly larger for the bases. Line the greased yorkshire pudding tins with
the larger rounds, put mincemeat in the centre, moisten edges of pastry with water. Put
the lids on, decorate edges. Make a hole in the centre of each one, with a skewer. Bake
for 25 mins on 425f 210c gas 7. Middle shelf. **Sprinkle with caster sugar and serve
hot or cold.**

Brandy Butter

125g butter, 75g icing sugar, brandy to taste

Beat the butter until soft, beat in the sugar. Add the brandy and mix well. Form into a
long roll in greaseproof paper and leave in the fridge to harden.
Cut off slices 5mm thick, when required.

Smoked Salmon

1. Serve the smoked salmon with cayenne pepper, lemon wedges and thinly-sliced brown bread and butter.

2. Serve the smoked salmon in small pastry cases (short crust pastry-see week 3) filled with soft cream cheese and freshly ground black pepper.

3. Serve together smoked salmon and potted prawns (see week 46) on a plate of crisp lettuce.

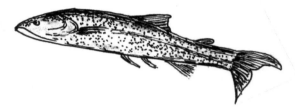

Bacon and Tomato Quiche

First make the short crust pastry – see week 3.
Filling:
175g bacon
1 onion
20g butter
3 eggs
300ml whipping cream
salt and pepper
150g cheddar cheese-grated
2 tomatoes-sliced

Roll out the pastry on a floured surface to 3mm thickness. Line a greased 9in flan case.
Slice the bacon and onion, fry together in butter for 10mins until cooked.
Cover the base of the pastry case with the cooked bacon and onion.
Beat the eggs, cream, salt, pepper and cheese together. Pour into the flan case.
Arrange the slices of tomato on top. Bake for 45 mins on 375f 190c gas 5 until golden brown. Middle shelf. **Serve hot or cold.**

Serves 6.

Chocolate log

75g self-raising flour
pinch of salt
30g drinking chocolate powder
1 tsp cocoa powder
75g butter
75g caster sugar
2 eggs
2-3 drops vanilla essence

Sieve the flour, salt, chocolate powder and cocoa powder altogether.
Beat the butter until soft, add the sugar and beat again until light and fluffy.
Mix in the eggs, one at a time with a tablespoon of flour, until all the dry ingredients are mixed in, add vanilla essence. Line a shallow baking tray with parchment paper [approx 12x10 inches]. Bake for 10 mins 425f 210c gas 7. Third shelf down.
Turn out, top downwards, onto sugared parchment paper. Trim off edges, roll up quickly with paper inside. When roll is cold, unroll carefully and spread with half the chocolate butter icing. Re-roll tightly. Cover outside and ends with rest of icing.
Decorate with a fork to resemble the bark of a tree, dust with icing sugar for a snow effect and put a robin on top.

Chocolate Butter Icing

60g dark chocolate
2 tbsp hot milk
90g unsalted butter
225g sifted icing sugar

Grate the chocolate into a bowl, add the hot milk and stir until the chocolate has melted.
Cream the butter and half the sugar together.
Add the melted chocolate and rest of sugar, mix together well. Use as required.

Shrimp and Cashew Nut Salad

450g cooked and peeled shrimps
3 tbsp mayonnaise
4 tbsp double cream
juice of ½ a lemon
salt and pepper
2 apples-peeled and sliced
1 celery heart-finely chopped
100g cashew nuts-toasted

Wash the shrimps under cold water, leave to drain.
Whisk the mayonnaise with the cream, add the lemon juice, salt and pepper to taste.
Mix in the shrimps, apples and celery.
Transfer the salad into a nice serving dish and decorate with the cashew nuts and celery leaves.

Serves 4.

Beef and Mushroom Pie

First make the short crust pastry – see week 3.
1 kg lean chuck steak
1 onion
200g button mushrooms
75g seasoned flour
3 tbsp vegetable oil
100g butter
1 pint stock
½ pint red wine
1 egg-beaten

Ask the butcher to trim and cut the beef into 1in dice pieces.
Peel, slice the onion and mushrooms. Roll the meat through seasoned flour.
Heat the oil, in a frying pan and fry the meat until evenly browned. Transfer the meat to a casserole. Melt the butter in the frying pan and cook the onion and mushrooms for 10 mins. Pour in the stock and wine, bring to the boil and pour over the meat. Cover the casserole with a lid and cook for 2 hours on 325f 165c gas 3. Middle shelf.
Allow the meat to cool, before making the pie. (continued on next page)

Beef and Mushroom Pie (continued)

To make the pie:
Divide the pastry in two halves. Roll out both on a floured surface, each to 4mm thickness. Line a greased 8in pie-dish with the first piece of pastry, trim around the edges. Place the beef and mushrooms inside the pie with a little of the gravy. Brush egg around the edges. Cover with the second piece of pastry, trim the edges and crimp down with fingers to seal. Make two slits for the steam to escape, brush over the top with egg. Bake for 25-30 mins on 425f 210c gas 7 until golden. Middle shelf.

Serves 6.

Cranberry Mousse

250g crème fraiche
250g double cream
200g frozen cranberries
80ml raspberry sauce – see week 29
80g caster sugar
3 leaves of gelatine
whipped cream

Place the gelatine in cold water for 10 mins.
Whisk the crème fraiche and cream together until thick.
Warm the cranberries slightly then crush with a fork, to burst each one. Heat gently, but not boiling.
Lift the gelatine out of the water, squeeze out excess water, stir into the cranberries until dissolved.
Allow to completely cool, then stir in the crème fraiche/double cream mixture.
Put into dessert glasses, leave in the fridge to set for at least 3 hours.
Decorate with whipped cream on top.

Serves 6.

Watercress Soup

30g butter, 1 onion-sliced, 2 bunches of watercress,
500g potatoes-chopped 1½ pints water, salt and pepper, 2 tbsp double cream

In a large saucepan, melt the butter and cook the onion for 5 mins. Trim the stalks from the watercress, peel and slice the potatoes and add them to the pan. Pour in the water and bring to the boil, simmer for 20 mins, until the potato is soft. Liquidize the soup to a smooth puree. Reheat and season to taste, stir in the cream to bind. **Serves 6.**

Turkey, roast

Turkey – 5.4 kg [12lbs] – dressed weight
soft butter, 300g streaky bacon

Put the bird in a large piece of foil. Rub over with butter, cover breast with bacon.
Wrap up the foil to make a parcel and place in a large roasting tin.
Roast 4-4½ hours on 330f 170c gas 3, removing foil and bacon for the last 30 mins to brown. Below middle shelf. Allow to rest before carving. **To make Thickened gravy – see week 6.**

Chestnut and Bacon Stuffing

1 onion-chopped	400g tin chestnut puree
100g bacon-chopped	1 egg
1 tbsp oil	100g breadcrumbs
450g pork sausage meat	pinch of nutmeg
2 tbsp dried mixed herbs	salt and pepper

In a frying pan, heat the oil and cook the onion with the bacon for 10 mins. In a bowl, mix all the ingredients together with the cooked onion and bacon. With a little flour on your hands, make the stuffing balls by rolling a small amount between the hands to form the shape. Bake for 20 mins on 400f 200c gas 6. Can be cooked in advance and reheated before serving the turkey.

Cranberry Sauce

150g apples, 150g cranberries, 150ml water, sugar to taste
Peel, quarter and core the apples. Stew the apples and cranberries in the water until soft. Mash to a pulp and sweeten to taste. **Serve with roast turkey or game.**

Bread Sauce

**1 onion studded with 3 cloves, pinch of nutmeg, 1 pint of milk,
125g white breadcrumbs, 30g butter, salt and pepper**

Put the onion and nutmeg into the milk, bring slowly to the boil. Simmer gently for 30 mins to infuse. Strain the milk and add the breadcrumbs and butter. Add salt and pepper to taste, simmer very slowly for another 20 mins. **Serve at once. Can be served with roast turkey or chicken.**

Christmas Pudding (makes 2 x 2lb puddings)

500g mixed dried fruit	**125g plain flour**
200g mixed peel	**60g self-raising flour**
rind and juice of 1 orange	**pinch of salt**
1 apple-peeled and diced	**75g breadcrumbs**
3 tbsp brandy	**2 eggs**
125g soft dark brown sugar	**few drops of almond essence**
200g vegetable suet	**½ cup of milk to bind**

In a bowl, soak the dried mixed fruit, mixed peel, rind and juice of 1 orange and the diced apple in the brandy for 1 hour. After 1 hour, stir in the sugar, suet, both the flours, salt, breadcrumbs, eggs, almond essence and milk to bind. Making the mixture to a dropping consistency. Grease two, 2 pint pudding basins. Scrap the mixture into the basins, using a spatula. Cover with greaseproof paper, tie string around the rim twice. Place the basin in a deep saucepan. Half fill the saucepan with boiling water and boil for 4 hours, topping up the water if it gets too low. When cooked, turn out onto a plate, cut into portions, decorate each one with a sprig of holly. If you are not using the pudding straight away, then store in a cool place until required. When required, reheat again in a saucepan of boiling water for 1½ hours before serving. **Serve with brandy sauce – see week 52. Serves 10.**

Brandy Sauce

1 pint milk, 60g butter, 60g plain flour, caster sugar to sweeten, brandy to flavour
Warm the milk and bring it slowly to simmering point. In another saucepan, melt the butter, add the flour and mix in well. Gradually stir in the milk, using a wooden spoon until all the milk has been incorporated. Gently simmer for 20 mins, do not allow the sauce to burn. Remove from heat, stir in the sugar to sweeten and enough brandy to taste. Strain through a fine sieve. Serve at once. The sauce can be made in advance and kept warm in a flask, until you are ready to serve.

Index

Index

Index

Index

Oven Temperatures

F	C	Gas Mark	Temperature
250	130	½	Very Cool
275	140	1	Very Cool
300	150	2	Cool
325	165	3	Warm
350	180	4	Moderate
375	190	5	Fairly hot
400	200	6	Fairly hot
425	215	7	Hot
450	230	8	Very Hot
475	240	9	Very hot

Where it mentions Stocks:
to save time you can use
a stock cube instead.

Weight

Metric	Imperial	Metric	Imperial
15g	½oz	425g	15oz
20g	¾oz	450g	1 lb
30g	1oz	500g	1 lb 2oz
60g	2oz	750g	1½ lb
90g	3oz	900g	2 lb
100g	3½oz	1kg	2 ¼ lb
120g	4oz	1.4kg	3 lb
150g	5oz	1.8kg	4 lb
175g	6oz	2.3kg	5 lb
200g	7oz	2.7kg	6 lb
225g	8oz	3.2kg	7 lb
250g	9oz	3.6kg	8 lb
300g	10oz	4.1kg	9 lb
325g	11oz	4.5kg	10 lb
350g	12oz	5.4kg	12 lb
375g	13oz	6.8kg	15 lb
400g	14oz